SOUTH CAMPUS LIBRARY
TARRANT COUNTY
JUNIOR COLLEGE
FT. WORTH, TEXAS 76119

SAUL BELLOW

By the same author

The Saul Bellow Estate (a memoir)
Not By Politics Alone ! (Edited with V.V. John)
Khushwant Singh (in press)

SAUL BELLOW

THE PROBLEM OF AFFIRMATION

CHIRANTAN KULSHRESTHA

ARNOLD-HEINEMANN

© Chirantan Kulshrestha
First Published 1978

Published by Gulab Vazirani for Arnold-Heinemann Publishers (India) Pvt. Ltd., AB/9, Safdarjang Enclave, New Delhi-110016 and printed by Sunil Composing Co. at S.P. Printers, New Delhi-110028.

Contents

	Introduction : The Territory Ahead	9
1.	Writing as a Mode of Affirmation	26
2.	Fictional Method	40
3.	The Victims	61
	Dangling Man	64
	Seize the Day	77
4.	The Adventurers	95
	The Adventures of Augie March	97
5.	The Survivors	108
	Herzog	114
	Mr. Sammler's Planet	132
	Conclusion : Toward a Mystique of Saul Bellow	150
	Notes	155
	Select Bibliography	163
	Index	173

Acknowledgements

To Saul Bellow and V.V. John for encouragement, sympathy, and understanding.

To George H. Mayer, Wayne C. Booth, S. Viswanathan, D.S. Maini, Nawal Kishore, Amritjit Singh, Isaac Sequeira, and J.N. Sharma for helpful criticism.

To Joel Porte, Gulab Vazirani, R.W.B. Lewis, Shiv K. Kumar, Suhasini Ramaswamy, S. Nagarajan, R.N. Mehta, and Dorothy Clark for interest and affection.

To the U.S. Educational Foundation in India and the Institute of International Education for a Fulbright-Smith-Mundt Fellowship (1970-71) to enable me to undertake research on Saul Bellow's fiction at the University of Chicago; the American Studies Research Centre, Hyderabad, for several study-grants; and the University of Udaipur for leave of absence (1969; 1970-71).

To the University of Hyderabad and the University Grants Commission for a generous publication-grant.

Abbreviations

DM : *Dangling Man*
TV : *The Victim*
SD : *Seize the Day*
AM : *The Adventures of Augie March*
HRK : *Henderson the Rain King*
H   : *Herzog*
SP : *Mr. Sammler's Planet*
HG : *Humboldt's Gift*

INTRODUCTION

The Territory Ahead

In the summer of 1971, on a visit to Stratford-on-Avon, I was particularly impressed by the intelligent and knowledgeable commentary provided by our tourist-guide. He was a tall, heavy, middle-aged Englishman with a weather-beaten face, a man not at all unusual in appearance and resembling the thousands who step out of the London fog every day in search of their fish and chips. What distinguished him was his creative use of language, the vivid and striking turns he unexpectedly gave to wooden details. I struck up a casual conversation with him, invited him to join me for a cup of tea, and was surprised to learn that he was a writer of children's stories. He worked as a guide during the tourist season to pursue his writing at leisure the rest of the year. He asked me what had brought me to England and appeared interested when I told him that I was returning from the United States after a year at the English Department of the University of Chicago. "So, you too are in the literary trade," he said connivingly, and asked for more details of the work I had done at Chicago.[1] On hearing that I had gone there to collect material on Saul Bellow's fiction and had had the opportunity of meeting the author, his interest increased even more. "Oh, you must have read all his novels, haven't you?" he asked me intently, "Have you read *Herzog*?" When I replied in the affirmative, he said: "You know something? *I am Herzog!*"[2]

It was my turn to be astonished. I reacted with skepticism and reservation. The man, I thought, was being theatrical and I wasn't going to allow him to practice his cheap and transparent guiles on me. He must have read my distrusting and partly hostile look, for he said: "Don't misunderstand me. I do not know Bellow: he has not heard of me and probably never will. What I meant was that I read *Herzog* at a very crucial time in my career. My life was going to seed. My wife suddenly announced one evening that she was going to leave me because she just couldn't continue living with me the way I was. Life then appeared to take on a dark hopeless look. When she left me finally, I found myself dangling between two equally undesirable options. If I committed suicide, I opted for total oblivion; if I chose to live the way I was, I saw another kind of meaninglessness staring me in the face. Well, I began reading this novel to divert myself and, in the process, found myself trying to piece together my life. It was like the counterbalancing of two different kinds of life-experiences—two alien lives in dialogue over matters of mutual interest. I realised that I just couldn't drift in time any more. I must be myself, recognise my calling, make sense of myself as a human being. You see, this is where the book helped me—to find coherence and peace, an understanding of my situation. So you see—*I am* Herzog !"[3]

As I boarded the Qantas flight at Heathrow Airport for New Delhi the following afternoon, my mind returned to my meeting with Stuart-Forbes, the guide at Stratford, and it seemed to me that in the quasi-symbolic setting of Shakespeare's birthplace I had unwittingly entered into a covenant with him. I saw myself as his neighbour in the Bellow Estate, experiencing the inescapable but characteristic tensions of Bellow's heroes, and trying desperately and earnestly to comprehend the enchanting muddle of the dream that is our existence. The Bellow Estate was, for me, a metaphor of my own peculiar anguished situation. Like Stuart-Forbes, I, then a young man of 24, had been obsessed with the problem of finding a proper vocation. I think now that I could have written to Bellow the kind of letter Herzog writes to Vinoba: "*I'd like to join your movement. I've always wanted very much to lead a moral, useful, and active life. I never knew where to begin.*" (*H*, p. 48).

By powerful invisible strings—the tug of which hurt where I breathed—I had been drawn to Bellow. In another country, born and grown to adulthood with different *samskaras*, I was trying to locate a personal centre of significance and often wondered if my soul really lay hidden in the pages of Bellow's novels. Sometimes I thought it was all wrong—that I was really a demon-haunted man struggling with the trappings of illusion in the palace of Circe. "Why should I, an Indian with modest pretensions to creative writing, be interested in Saul Bellow, an American novelist?" I frequently asked myself and tried to reason why aspects of his fiction should appeal so movingly to my Hindu mind. The first of these questions was posed to me innumerable times—in India and in the United States—and as my work on Bellow progressed over the wintry months in Chicago, I cultivated clever, defensive, reflex answers that I myself did not believe in—broad, nonspecific, witty answers that referred to the rise of American Studies in India and of the opportunistic advantage of producing a quick dissertation on a relatively less researched author. When I mentioned these questions to Bellow in one of our meetings, he himself added an answer to my list by remarking that twentieth-century literature had become so international that there was nothing to be surprised at in an Indian's interest in a contemporary American writer.[4]

Bellow, I felt, was merely rationalising a foreigner's interest in his work. His answer was not my answer, though at that time he was among the few people with whom I shared closeness and warmth. I sensed that my work on Bellow was intimately and mysteriously related to the problem of my own intellectual identity, and yet I was unable to figure out the answer in terms that would be intelligible to other people.

The answer came to me unexpectedly at the close of a sitting with Bellow. I was trying to pin him down to a firm and concrete statement on the Jewish quality of his work, and he was vehemently repulsing the overture, calling the Jewish tag "false and wrong." True enough, Bellow had never undertaken to plead the "Jewish case" and yet his work had a resonance and a strength—shall I say, a flavour or a nuance?—which seemed unmistakably Jewish. The twist of an argument, the bittersweet anecdote, at times the assertion of a traditional and old-fashioned stance that writers unsure of their cultural and religious roots would not normally hazard—these qualities did not seem to square up with his spirited denial of conscious ethnicity. Suddenly I felt that Bellow was trying to convey a meaning that was perhaps transverbal and complex, because it was intensely personal and involved. I wondered if he was a Jew as I was a Hindu—secularised on the surface under the pressure of modern life and yet so vitally joined to a reservoir of cultural energy that our spirituality became unconsciously absorbed in the way we felt, thought, talked, acted, and related ourselves to people. Could Bellow—a Jew, a writer, an elderly friend—clarify for me the creative problems I had, as a Hindu, as a younger writer struggling to produce, besides other things, a sort of work of fiction? The question formed itself spontaneously in my mind—I think I have been rarely so naive and so truthful. "As one with some pretensions to creative writing I want advice from you," I said to him, "I am a Hindu, a secularised Hindu. I don't go to temples or sit in worship, but there is a way of life that comes to me naturally, which I cannot avoid, which is very much a part of my being, and which I cannot but call Hindu. There is much in the Hindu way of life that fascinates me with its creative possibilities, but much that would appear irrational to the scientific mind. Writing about that seems such a risk, a step in darkness."[5]

Bellow reacted to the question with a tenderness I had not anticipated. It was, I like to think, one of those moments when truths get uttered without the taints of irony or ambivalence. "You should take a risk," he said, "you should take a chance. What I would say to this is simply that your imagination in its most open days was formed by the Hindu religion. How could you possibly repudiate or renounce that? Your mind takes its colour from this and it is one of the great gifts of your life. For whom should you repudiate this? You should not repudiate it for anybody. It's part of the power of your imagination by now and so you should cherish it as such. Not as belief, not to defend against rational argument or by rational argument, but simply as a fact of your life. For it is a fact of your life. *That's how I view my own Jewishness.* That's where the great power of it comes from. It doesn't come from the fact that I studied the *Talmud,* or anything of that sort. I never belonged to an orthodox congregation. It simply comes from the fact that at a most susceptible time of my life I was wholly Jewish. That's a gift, a piece of good fortune with which one doesn't quarrel."[6]

As I walked home that afternoon from Bellow's office, my

mind was in a whirl. I was not sure if I had refined out of my confusions a statement that would make sense to others. *That* was hardly my problem. My mind had seized the clue Bellow had offered, and connections were gradually becoming perceptible. I was beginning to see that the situation of a writer like Bellow was one without alternatives. It was not for him to opt for or opt out of his Jewishness. The choices were made for him at the most receptive time of his life, in the way he had grown up: to use his lexicon, they were a fact of his life, a given. For him Jewishness was not a tool of propaganda; it could not be exploited for the gain of committed interests. It was a felt experience that gave his work its special slant and colour, its speech-rhythms, and its increasingly pronounced moral tones. It provided the esthetic context in which his particular problems and priorities as a creative artist could be understood and explained.

I could now account for my involvement with Bellow in more coherent terms. I was drawn to his work because he seemed the artist from whom I could learn the creative uses of language and experience. I did not wish to imitate or follow him; that would have been superficial and mindless. I sought to make use of him as he had made use of Dostoevski, Dreiser, and Mann. I could see how one's native and innate resources of language and experience could be significantly exploited and preserved in an artifact that affirmed the vitality of tradition on the one hand and revalued contemporary styles of expression and thought on the other. In my reading of contemporary literature I knew of no writer who had accomplished this as competently and eloquently as Saul Bellow.

My desire to watch the artist with his chisel and hammer led me to the Joseph Regenstein Library at the University of Chicago where the Saul Bellow papers are deposited. I found the papers classified into four basic categories. Series A and D contained correspondence and mementos; series B and C included manuscripts, galley proofs, holographs and other papers relating to Bellow's major and minor work, published as well as unpublished. One discovers here, for example, that in 1940

Bellow undertook to write an ovel, provisionally titled *Actala*, which he never completed. The hard work that made *The Adventures of Augie March*, *Henderson the Rain King*, and *Herzog* possible can also be evidenced in the large number of notebooks and drafts representing the different stages through which these novels evolved before publication. To take a random instance, of *Herzog* there exist 27 notebooks, each displaying some growth in situation, theme, and character-delineation. Notebook I introduces Moses Herzog as Amram Herzog, as a physicist interested in the humanities. By Notebook 16 he becomes an ethnologist, and, in the typed draft B: 18: 17, the author of a textbook *Contemporary Humanities*. Luke Asphalter, presented as Axel Johannes in an earlier draft, acquires greater intellectual and emotive sensitivity in successive versions of the novel, but, as against the original figure's dressy and immaculate presence, becomes slovenly in appearance. Other manuscripts also contain such interesting changes and revisions.

When told that the use of certain items in the collection required prior permission, I sought Bellow's reason for not permitting researchers to inspect his unpublished and abandoned manuscripts. Bellow remarked that the discarded projects were like the miscarriages of women and he saw no reason why anyone should be interested in them.

What could have been merely an encounter with a number of ghostly versions of a text sometimes turned into a source of fresh insights as I rummaged through the Bellow papers. In one of the folders of *The Future of the Moon* (published subsequently as *Mr. Sammler's Planet*), I discovered accidentally a file containing the papers, some published, others still in the form of drafts, of Bellow's friend Edward Shils, the eminent sociologist. Since the novel does carry several speculations of a sociological nature, it was not entirely pointless to wonder if Bellow had been assisted, to some degree, by Shils. Bellow was startled when I mentioned Shils's file. He said that it must have got into the folder by mistake and that he must see to its removal at once. I wonder if the file is still there.

What was poignantly revealed to me during my contact with

Saul Bellow and my perusal of his manuscripts, folders, and holographs was his anxious concern with the moral determinants of his vocation. Convinced of the bankruptcy of the systematic certainties provided by ideologies, he has endeavoured to explore the contours of those marginal free spaces where human and artistic significances may reside. For literature there are no other alternatives, he says: "If there is no significant space, there is no judgment, no freedom, we determine nothing for ourselves individually."[7] Bellow's affirmative vision has always had the advantage of an ever ripening creativity sustained in a career spanning over thirty years by a consistently enriching awareness of the relevance of the human soul to the craft of the writer and the extended world of practical affairs. He claims that writers cannot hope to become interesting by trying to command power in the political sense, but by tapping "an inadmissible resource, something we all hesitate to mention though we all know it intimately—the soul."[8] The novelist's business, he insists, is to spurn the trite "formulae of modern intelligence" and to write with "the natural knowledge of the soul," without preconceptions, without overtly trying to plead or prove a case. The sense of liberation one encounters in his fiction results from his refusal to commit himself to any political cause or religious dogma and is primarily responsible for his survival—and occupancy—in a highly competitive literary market which has witnessed the gradual exhaustion of the talents of writers such as J.D. Salinger, William Burroughs, Philip Roth, Truman Capote, James Baldwin, Normal Mailer, and Bernard Malamud. Bellow's innate discipline—issuing from a unique blend of intellectual astuteness and subtle craftsmanship—has helped him escape such a predicament, and if his recent novels (*Herzog, Mr. Sammler's Planet*, and *Humboldt's Gift*) have all been prize-winners, it is because they represent the maturation of artistic possibilities that are evident in his work right from the start.

Although the increasing bulk of scholarship on Saul Bellow has begun to approach the proportions of a minor industry, the responses of most critics have been limited by their inability to consider his novels in the context of his problems as a practising writer.[9] As a result, they have been concerned not so much with his preoccupation with the *problem* of affirmation as with an interpretation of his novels in terms of the categories of optimism and pessimism, hope and despair, joy and suffering, alienation and togetherness, good and evil, and so on. It is true that affirmation cannot at any point be subtracted from these categories, but it is nonetheless important to take note of the creative anxiety or the pressure on artistic sensibility that invariably accounts for a writer's affirmative choices. Bellow's critics overlook the fact that affirmation for him has always been a source of persistent anxiety and that his attempts to clarify and define its numerous ramifications have moulded his fictional method. They fail to perceive that the contradictions they report in his work are not in the nature of a defect but are welded together by his creative anxiety and reflect his deep concern with the various allied and conflicting issues that compete for a writer's attention in the artistic process. This, if anything, is the source of the "intelligence" that Tony Tanner praises but seldom probes in Bellow's fiction.[10] The gap between the tenor and the vehicle that he notices in the novels appears superficial because the esthetic priorities at the back of Bellow's anxiety ultimately become instrumental in shaping the specifics of his method. In fact, the tenor and the vehicle are so inextricably interlinked in Bellow's case that the only available means to make sense of the problematic character of his affirmation is to isolate the important ways in which his anxiety struggles for articulation in his novels. Such an approach requires that the emphasis be shifted from affirmed categories to the fictional process or method that leads to these categories. The pre-eminence to be accorded to the process or method also implies that the operative word in the conceptual formulation of this study be *problem* rather than affirmation. Since an attempt has been made in this book to view the latter largely in terms of the former, no need has been felt to begin with a preconceived or conclusive definition of affirmation within whose steel-frame the meanings of the novels may be conscripted. It has been found sufficient to present Bellow's reactions to the commonplace notions of affirmation in order to connote the nature of the problem he confronts. The resolution of the problem is apprehended through the method he employs in his novels to dramatise the plight of his protagonists. Special attention has been devoted to the analysis of the protagonists' experience and consciousness in the light of narrative devices and strategies so that it may be possible to determine the extent to which Bellow's craftsmanship is put to use in qualifying and limiting his modes of affirmation.

Chapter 1 discusses Bellow's anxiety concerning the necessity of affirmation and the role of the artist in modern society in relation to the stances of the first and second generation writers of the twentieth-century. The first generation writers sidestepped the question of affirmation by assuming a hostile attitude to life and by consciously seeking solace in the world of art. The second generation writers did not consider art an adequate substitute for life, but their work gave ample testimony to their belief that modern society represented the perversion and decay of man's finest hopes. Bellow shares the faith of the first generation writers in the power of art, but refuses to admit any opposition between art and life. Art divorced from life, in his view, becomes subjective; its contact with life invigorates it with a sense of truth. He shows an acute awareness of the ills of society, but denies that it is doomed. Artists must recover, he maintains, from their attitudes of "unearned bitterness," human qualities may appear suppressed in modern society but they still exist, and artists have to look with their own eyes to discover them anew and make a clear estimate of the human condition.

The artist's role is made particularly difficult in America, says Bellow, because the mass-media enter into competition with him and abrogate his authority. The artist must, therefore, do something that the media cannot do. He must act as the conscience of the community and try to restore through art the wonder and enchantment of life that industrial and technological forces have tended to blur and dissipate. He must justify life because it is in itself a negation of non-being. Since writing helps the artist exercise his authority for the celebration of life, it is an act of faith, a gesture of caring for others, in essence, a mode of affirmation.

Chapter 2 deals with Bellow's anxiety to adopt a fictional method that may express his reservations about the kind of affirmation he regards unsatisfactory at the same time as it may realise the modes of affirmation he cherishes. This anxiety is reflected in Bellow's novels in various exclusions which suggest, through dramatised fictional events, his esthetic preferences and priorities. Bellow's novels give a clear indication of his skepticism of the modes of affirmation based on (i) a naive belief in the essential unity of mankind; (ii) the cult of the ego with its trust in the ultimate value of experience and its rejection of ordinariness and finitude; and (iii) abstract, metaphysical attempts to construe the nature of reality. Bellow employs Socratic irony to highlight and, at times, correct the errors of his protagonists and to retain an open attitude to the conclusions at which they arrive. The method combines intellectual and religious approaches in its reliance on the spirit of reason as well as the power of intuition. It supports and continues overtly intellectual stances about human life to a point where they discredit themselves, leaving behind, as an alternative, a system of ethical and religious values that affirm the promise of a fulfilled life.

Bellow's method is analysed in terms of the thematic and technical particularities of five selected novels in *Chapter 3*, *Chapter 4*, and *Chapter 5*. The chapters, entitled respectively "The Victims," "The Adventurers," and "The Survivors," stand for the three broad divisions under which these novels have been placed for studying the increasing seriousness with which Bellow grapples with the problem of affirmation. The chapter-titles refer to the "psychic portraits" of Bellow's protagonists. Although all Bellow heroes possess certain common traits, it is possible to draw dividing lines to distinguish one kind of temperament from another. The sublimation of "The Victims" (Joseph, Leventhal, Wilhelm) through "The Adventurers" (Augie, Henderson) into "The Survivors" (Herzog, Sammler, and Citrine) represents a marked refinement of sensibility and consciousness: from Joseph to Citrine, Bellow's protagonists show a consistent attempt to outgrow their feeling that life is without pattern and move over to a position where they can exercise choices discriminately, acquire an awareness of their own significance, and affirm their faith in purposive values. "The Victims" are insecure and recalcitrant, unwilling to assume responsibility, and suspicious of their fellowmen. Even when they succeed in liberating themselves from their problems, their release appears less an act of will than the result of an unexpected coincidence. "The Adventurers," in comparison, display a greater exuberance. They accept their responsibility toward others and possess the instinct to preserve their freedom by declining to be tempted by their Reality Instructors. They visualise the possibility of a fulfilled life, but hover on its borders, never fully realising it but also never giving up hope. "The Survivors" reject victimhood and cultivate a morality typical of people who have been exposed to suffering and pain. Their anguished awareness of the actuality of life's problems denies them a temperamental cheerfulness, but their acceptance of finitude and ordinariness gives them the strength to overcome their crises. They are, thus, able to go beyond their own explanations of reality and the persuasive lifestyles of their Reality Instructors to find contentment in a state of being at repose in contradictions and sustained by a faith in God.

Since the three-fold division of the novels is intended to correspond to Bellow's developing concern with the problem of affirmation, it is essentially chronological. The sole exception is the inclusion of *Seize the Day* in the category of the victim-novels — and not without some justification. The publication of this novella in 1956, after *The Adventures of Augie March* (1953) and before *Henderson the Rain King* (1959), makes for a thematic incongruity in Bellow's development as a novelist which has never been satisfactorily explained. Ray B. West[11] and Leslie A. Fiedler,[12] who were among the earliest critics to note that the novella had greater affinities with *Dangling Man* (1944) and *The Victim* (1947), Bellow's first two novels, than with *Augie March* and *Henderson the Rain King*, made no effort to probe the nature of the discontinuity and conveniently rationalised it as an evidence of Bellow's "return" to the closed-in world of the early novels. Another example of the distorted view of Bellow's development resulting from a complacent reliance on the novella's year of publication can be seen in Helen Weinberg's hasty attempt to bracket Joseph, Leventhal, and Wilhelm, the protagonists of *Dangling Man*, *The Victim*, and *Seize the Day*, with Augie. Weinberg maintains that Wilhelm, "although a victim-hero who may be viewed in the light of the two earliest novels nevertheless occurs in a novella written after *Augie March* and can be regarded as much an extension of the new view that *Augie March* represents as another manifestation of the victim-hero."[13] The confusion at the heart of Weinberg's remark is typical of most of Bellow's representative critics who either offer ingenious interpretations to account for the anachronistic placement of *Seize the Day* or ignore the problem altogether. As a result, the novella continues to occupy an odd and ill-fitting place in the Bellow chronology.

A perusal of the Saul Bellow papers deposited with the Joseph Regenstein Library at the University of Chicago led me to surmise that *Seize the Day* may not have been written in the period immediately preceding its publication. As in the case of *Dangling Man* and *The Victim*, there is not enough early manuscript material available to help a conclusive identification of the period when it was first begun. The one holograph and four typewritten drafts of the novella held by the Humanities Research Centre at the University of Texas also offer no illumination in the matter. In comparison, there is no dearth of early notebooks of *Augie March*—publication-wise the predecessor of *Seize the Day—Henderson the Rain King*, *Herzog*, *Mr. Sammler's Planet*, and *Humboldt's Gift*. This enforces the by no means positive probability that *Seize the Day* belongs with *Dangling Man* and *The Victim* to a period when Bellow took little care to preserve his working drafts; otherwise, the resource material on the novella would certainly have been available with that on the later novels.

Interestingly enough, some notes on Wilhelm and his father are to be found at the back of notebook C : 1 : 9 of the Saul Bellow Papers placed in the Joseph Regenstein Library. The notebook also contains an undated draft of an early fragment entitled "Memoirs of a Bootlegger's Son," which was eventually incorporated in *Herzog*. This fact, by itself, is not accidental and provokes speculation. "Memoirs of a Bootlegger's Son," as included in *Herzog*, presents a moving account of Jonah Herzog, the protagonist's father and his hostility toward his son. The hostility develops from the old man's reluctance to underwrite his son's expenses (*H*, pp. 247-248). In *Seize the Day*, Wilhelm's bitterness is also partly due to this failure to persuade his father to help him. Both Herzog and Wilhelm are in the midst of a serious domestic crisis when they approach their fathers for money. Both have extra-marital affairs with Catholic girls, and there is a striking similarity in the details recalled by both of the mornings when their girls prepared to go to the church (*SD*, p. 94; *H*, p. 110). In *Herzog*, the details are considerably enlarged and vivid as compared to the fleeting glimpses of the same event in *Seize the Day*. Also, it is possible to locate in the novella the origin of Bellow's view that an individual's excessive preoccupation with his problems gives him a theatrical appearance. Wilhelm is told by his father not to "carry on like an opera" and make a "career" of his suffering, and Herzog, finding his rival giving a loving bath to his daughter, realises that his bitter thoughts about revenge have "turned into *theatre*, into something ludicrous" (*SD*. pp. 45-49; *H*, p. 258). Such obvious resemblances suggest that it is not entirely improbable that the novella and the novel were initially conceived by Bellow as parts of a single theme. He started work on it early in his career, suspended and interrupted it to devote his energy to other novels, and finally decided to make use of it in a novella and a novel when he found that it contained possibilities that did not exactly converge on a single character and situation and could be better exploited in two different works.

It is not difficult to see what motivated Bellow to make this crucial choice. If the theme was conceived in the period preceding the publication of *Augie March*, it was natural for the protagonist to partake of the qualities of the victim-hero. Wilhelm is continually oppressed by his problems and discerns no pattern or value in life. Like Joseph and Leventhal, he regards himself as an inhabitant of an inhuman world where meaningful communication and relationships are rendered impossible by selfishness, suspicion, and cynicism. He takes sedatives to soothe his nerves and desperately prays to God for mercy. But, like other victim-heroes, he is denied religious grace by the limited insight he has into his situation. By mourning the death of a stranger, he checks his excessive involvement with his problems and makes a gesture of identification with all men. His sudden release justifies the position of *Seize the Day* at the tail-end of the victim-group, suggesting not only a relationship but also an advance.

Seize the Day shares other affinities with *Dangling Man* and *The Victim*. It displays the same meticulous attention to technique and structure that is characteristic of the early novels. Bellow extends in *Seize the Day* the experiment with the first and third person points of view that he had made in *Dangling Man* and *The Victim*, and achieves effects mainly through a compact narrative organisation. The "adventure-novels," on the other hand, create precisely the opposite impression: as a first hand account of experience, they rely on the I-narrator; their narrative is fluid and sprawling, and the effects are deliberately diffused. Beside, Bellow approaches Leventhal's growing maturity and Wilhelm's involuntary transcendence *structurally* through virtually identical processes of self revelation. At critical moments in their crisis, Leventhal and Wilhelm are exposed to the sight of crowds to bring them the awareness that they are not exceptional in suffering and share with mankind its hopes and sorrows. The images of the crowds in the two books derive from the second epigraph to *The Victim* borrowed from De Quincey's *The Pains of Opium*:

> Be that as it may, now it was that upon the rocking waters of the ocean the human face began to reveal itself; the sea appeared paved with innumerable faces, upturned to the heavens; faces, imploring, wrathful, despairing; faces that surged upward by thousands, by myriads, by generations...

In a parallel image in *Seize the Day* the feelings behind the "imploring, wrathful, despairing" faces are identified as a collectivity of human strivings:

> And the great, great crowd, the inexhaustible current of millions of every race and kind pouring out, pressing round, of every age, of every genius, possessors of every human secret, antique and future, in every face the refinement of one particular motive or essence—*I labor, I spend, I strive, I design, I love, I cling, I uphold, I give way, I envy, I long, I scorn, I die, I hide, I want*. Faster, much faster than any man could make the tally (*SD*, p. 115).

These remarks about the genesis of *Seize the Day* are by no means conclusive, but they do make a case for its inclusion in the victim-group and raise an honest doubt about the actual period of its composition. In an interview with me, Bellow himself acknowledged the validity of this guesswork and agreed that *Seize the Day* was "very much like *The Victim*." The relevant dialogue is reproduced below:

> *Interviewer*: Now a question relating to a personal problem. I have always had trouble "placing" *Seize the Day*. Although chronologically it appears in 1956, between *The Adventures of Augie March* (1963) and *Henderson the Rain King* (1959), I have been more inclined to group it with *Dangling Man* (1944) and *The Victim* (1947). The justification is both formal and thematic; it is as tightly organised as the first two novels, and, in spite of its make-up of a victim novel, it moves to a very unexpected transcendence, suggesting thus a relationship with and an advance on the victim-group. Could I have your clarification?
>
> *Bellow*: That's right. That's very shrewd, an excellent observation. That's the way I think of it myself. You are very right. It really is true that Wilhelm belongs to the victim-group.
>
> *Interviewer*: My own feeling was that the novel was written earlier and held over, but I had no way of proving that...
>
> *Bellow*: Well, it was written over a period of years and I don't remember now when it was begun. You may be right even about it. However, I have long since done with that. It wasn't written in the same mood, but the state of mind is similar. *Seize the Day* is victim literature, very much like *The Victim* itself... [14]

An important mode of affirmation that this study leaves out of discussion relates to the Jewishness of Bellow's work. The reason for omitting a discussion of such a vital source of creativity is located in my unfamiliarity with Judaism and my feeling that an alien critical idiom is often inherently illequipped to analyse nuances developing out of the cultural, ethnic, and religious influences that are unselfconsciously absorbed by a writer during his upbringing and apprenticeship. Besides, even among the more sensitive of Bellow's Jewish critics, there appears to be no acceptable consensus on the expression of Judaism in his fiction. In his study of the crisis of identity and assimilation among American Jewish writers, Allen Guttmann does little more than provide intelligent summaries to bring out the Jewish quality of Bellow's novels.[15] Irving Malin, another sympathetic Jewish critic, finds "Bellow's view of his heritage" essentially ambivalent: "he may use Jewish vision—or irony—but he never confronts it . . . except by indirection. Often he avoids it—by masquerading it as something else."[16] According to Robert Alter, the influence of Judaism on writers like Bellow and Malamud "is for the most part peculiarly tangential, however conspicuous it may sometime be in their work."[17] Bellow himself has reacted vehemently to the "Jewish label" and called it "false and wrong":

> One has one's character—a given—and that's it. He had better be faithful to the given and if other people don't like it that's unfortunate. I have never consciously written as a Jew. I have just written as Saul Bellow. I have never attempted to make myself Jewish, I've never tried to appeal to a community, I never thought of writing for Jews exclusively. I never wanted to. I think of myself as a person of Jewish origin—American and Jewish—who has had a certain experience of life, which is in part Jewish. Proportions are not for me to decide. I don't know what they are: how much is Jewish, how much is Russian, how much is male, how much twentieth-century, how much is midwestern. That's for others to determine with their measuring sticks. I have no sticks myself.[18]

Bellow's reluctance in acknowledging the Jewish quality of his fiction reminds one of Harold Rosenberg's comment that it is not uncommon for Jewish artists to feel intrigued and embarrassed by enquiries about the creative projection of their ethnicity. To the question, "Is there a Jewish art?" says Rosenberg, "there is a Gentile answer and a Jewish answer. The Gentile answer is: Yes, there is a Jewish art, and No, there is no Jewish art. The Jewish answer is: What do you mean by Jewish art?"[19]

A sensible way of resolving the problem is to go beyond

the simplistic categories of the hypothetical Gentile answer that Rosenberg mocks and to view Bellow's attitude to his Jewish heritage as a *personal anxiety* which makes it incumbent on him to escape its parochial character and discover significant creative outlets in fictional situations. Such an approach, though desirable, is not, however, easily accessible to a literary criticism that gives primacy to the explication of texts and, therefore, eludes and baffles critics—even the Jewish critics. Its proper study belongs, perhaps, to the realms of biography and theology. This book does not intrude in these realms and is content to accept the limits it has drawn around itself: it is essentially confined to a consideration of the problem of affirmation as an anxiety manifested in the method Bellow employs in his novels, though it does recognise that a fuller understanding of Bellow's ethnic background would undoubtedly deepen the appreciation of his work. That task, unfortunately, belongs to an entirely different area of investigation and calls for an equipment and erudition beyond the scope of this book.

CHAPTER 1

Writing as a Mode of Affirmation

Terms such as affirmation and commitment have generally aroused the suspicion of modern writers. They are taken to imply an acceptance of a given world-view or an ideology and its conscious celebration in art. It is assumed that they stifle creativity by imposing pre-fabricated structures of belief on the imagination and, consequently, encourage smugness and complacence. Gustave Flaubert, whose influence on twentieth-century fiction is an accredited commonplace of literary history, indicated his preference for an art freed of moral stances and asserted that "An artist must be in his work like God in creation... everywhere felt, but nowhere seen."[1] James Joyce cherished the ideal of esthetic objectivity and believed that the artist "remains within or behind or beyond or above his handiwork, invisible, refined out of existence, indifferent, paring his fingernails."[2] T.S. Eliot maintained that in poetry "that which is to be communicated is the poem itself, and only incidentally the experience and the thought which have gone into it."[3] Emphasising the need to purge the novel of all the elements that were extraneous to it, André Gide complained that the novel had missed "that deliberate avoidance of life, which gave style to the works of the Greek Dramatists."[4]

These examples suggest that some of the most influential writers of the twentieth-century bypassed the question of affirmation by taking shelter in a protective aestheticism. In their devotion to art, they sought support from the doctrine of impersonality, but did not directly confront the problem of art's relationship with life. It may even be said that these writers retreated from life and discovered in art their greatest consolation. Erich Auerbach points out that in the first generation of twentieth-century writers "there is something hostile to the reality which they represent . . . a turning away from the practical will to live, or delight in portraying it under its most brutal forms. There is a hatred of culture and civilization, brought out by means of the subtlest stylistic devices which culture and civilization have developed."[5] Extending Auerbach's argument, R.W.B. Lewis claims that the disdain of life found in Joyce, Mann, Proust, and Virginia Woolf was in answer to the universal pressure of death on modern historic life from all sides—"death in battle, death in prison, death in the pit of the soul and the very heart of the culture."[6] To these writers, art appeared the sole channel of approaching a living reality: "Turning away, therefore, from the City of Man, which was dying, the writer of that time entered alone into the deathless City of Art."[7]

Saul Bellow shares the distrust of his distinguished predecessors—the first generation writers of the twentieth-century—in the concepts of affirmation and commitment. He also shares their dedication to art. But unlike them, and in common with his immediate predecessors, the second generation writers such as Camus, Faulkner, Malraux, Silone, and Moravia, he holds that the art cannot be a substitute for life.[8] Life or reality, for Bellow, is intractable and mysterious; it steps beyond intellectual systems and resists all conceptions about itself; it cannot, therefore, be exchanged for art. Such a conviction also sets him apart from the second generation of modern writers whose view of life is permeated with a sense of loss. Bellow does not accept Camus' conception of man's cosmic homelessness or Faulkner's nostalgia for "a period of innocence and honor, humility and pride" that is now irrevocably lost.[9] To Bellow, such attitudes are an outcome of the writer's obsessive disgust with ordinary reality. Convinced that a trust in a lost paradise is illusory and often the source of the modern writer's despair, Bellow feels that ordinary life has always been man's true condition and that its exclusion from art is a step toward inauthenticity and error. In his own work, art and life exist not as opposites but as complementaries. A typical illustration of the delicate and necessary relationship he perceives between art and life can be found in his response to a question concerning the affirmative quality of his novel *Mr. Sammler's Planet*. Asked directly if the novel did not contradict his earlier warning against "Affirmation and Life Affirmers—the princes of the big time . . . who whoop it up for life," Bellow stated that he was "interested neither in affirming nor denying anything."[10] His important concern was not with the communication of a personal message, but with the internal logic of the novel:

> A "character" has his own logic. He goes his way, one goes with him; he has some perceptions, one perceives them with him. You do him justice, you don't grind your axe. I have no axe to grind, one way or the other. This man seemed to me to be the sort of man to whom this would be happening: he happens to have religious feelings. I did not choose such a person for the purpose of expressing my own religious convictions. I was simply following the thread of his being. I found a clue and I was winding it up, going inwards. It brought me to religion. If it had brought me elsewhere, I'd have written something else. One doesn't arbitrarily invent these things in order to put anything across. That's what I am trying to say to you.[11]

This statement rejects the popular notion of affirmation and asserts the neutrality and authority vital to the writer's craft. At the same time, it points to the link that brings art and life together in a significant relationship. In his Nobel Prize acceptance lecture, Bellow identifies this link with a sense of truth.[12] A writer's commitment to his art, he seems to be saying, is indistinguishable from his commitment to truth. Truth is the corrective force that gives balance to a writer's work, checks him from grinding his own axe, and modifies the extremes of an excessively interiorized view of life. The competence of a writer is determined by his ability to "pay particular attention to the subtleties of a particular case"[13] and not by his dogmatic and uncritical acceptance of fashionable stances or world-views. Bellow, thus, presupposes no alienation between art and life. The autonomy he grants the artist is not anterior to life but relies on a sense of truth to delineate with intimate nearness the being of a character and to preserve, in the process, the objectivity indispensable to a writer's pursuit of his vocation.

The sense of truth Bellow values in the relationship of art and life governs his approach to the problem of affirmation. He recognises that the affirmation offered by a writer to appease an eager reading public often distorts and conceals truth. Stale and unoriginal, it turns into "an endorsement of the status quo, an approving acceptance of this commercial civilization of ours."[14] Sometimes in reacting against an ideology of false optimism, the writer swings to the opposite extreme of the ideology of exaggerated wretchedness. It is believed, says Bellow in an obvious reference to Leslie Fiedler, that the writer should conform to "a negative tradition, a tradition of fire and sword, a tradition of prophetic denunciation" and say no powerfully "in the accents of thunder."[15] Bellow considers it possible that a writer may be led in the course of his work, "as an inevitable consequence of what he was writing," to take up an essentially negative stance. But if he deliberately strives to assume this moral attitude, then he is likely to be a humbug because "anything not related to the writer's passion simply produces false art."[16] And then, the "art of the novel itself has a dreadful tendency to oppose the conscious or ideological purpose of the writer. The laws of art occasionally ruin the most constructive intentions."[17] If a writer is going to be affirmative

> he must be prepared to demonstrate his affirmation in close detail, he must illustrate or prove his thesis with hard facts, and these facts are very often stubborn, refractory things, very hard to get under control. They have a way of biting the hand that manipulates them.[18]

Bellow believes that affirmation is really not a matter of choice for the writer: it is implicit in the act of writing. He cites the example of Flaubert who was solemnly commited to "objective seriousness" and yet created the realistic novel in its modern form with perceptive insights into the problems of nineteenth-century French bourgeois culture. The inescapable conclusion is that "it is impossible to touch the world even for art's sake without opening unknown, unseen, reserves of feeling, realms of passion."[19] Writing is, therefore, an act of faith, a moral necessity. By caring about the people whom he fictionalizes, the writer manifests his belief in the existence of others: "this caring or believing or love alone matters" and constitutes the writer's commitment to life.[20] Bellow denies that the writer's sovereignty is in any way compromised by his commitment to life and visualises for art a role that is fully consistent with its moral intones. He conceives of art as "a purgation of consciousness"[21] having "something to do with the achievement of stillness in the midst of chaos. A stillness which characterizes prayer."[22] His conception of himself in the creative act is like that of a medium receptive to a source of inspiration and truth whom he chooses to identify as a "primitive commentator." The commentator is primitive not because he is crude but because he is uncompromising: a ground has to be prepared before he can be made to tell "what the real world is."[23] The prompter must find the occasion perfect—"that is to say, truthful, and necessary"—in order to function with optimum efficiency: "If there is any superfluity or inner falsehood in the preparation he is aware of it. I have to stop. Often I have to begin again, with the first word."[24]

Bellow's reliance on the primitive commentator to cleanse his art of distortions, impurities, and untruth helps to clarify his own problems as a writer. He notes the changed attitude of the writer to his vocation in modern society and wonders if it has not been for the worse. From the middle of the nineteenth-century writers have sought to be more than writers: "they have been their own theoreticians, have created their own ground as artists, and have provided an exegesis for their own works. They have found it necessary to take a position, not merely to write novels."[25] By turning themselves into cultural institutions and publicists, artists have lost the humility and modesty that comes from a knowledge of one's obscurity and insignificance. Their art has also suffered in the bargain because the energy of art intrinsically depends on the freedom and peace emanating from the artists's confident acceptance of limits in private and professional spheres. In Bellow's creative process the authority of the primitive commentator pre-determines an attitude of self-criticism and humility and necessarily enforces a regard for truth. His insistence on the primitive or ancient character of his prompter reinforces his contention that the great imperative for art is to dissociate itself from theoretical abstractions and ingenious explanations of reality and try to restore the magic or enchantment of life—the sense of strangeness of life innate in every human being—which has vanished due to the industrial, technical and rational revolutions.[26]

The obstacles attending the realisation of such a vision in art constitute for Bellow the essence of the problem of affirmation. In his frame of reference, the problem is confronted not as an equation involving the simplistic categories of optimism or pessimism, hope or despair, good or evil, or as a literary programme to be executed to the letter. "I've seen a great many optimistic rackets in my time," he says, "and I've seen a good many pessimistic rackets; and I don't believe that I should be a demagogue and try to win favour by expressing popular points of view."[27] He rejects "the idiocy of orthodox affirmation" as also the despair and hopelessness provoked by "transparent or pointless optimism."[28] To him the problem of affirmation is above and beyond particular stances or world-views: it is an aspect of the problems of the creative writer, a pressure on the writer's sensibility that determines the mode of existence of his work. It is intimately related to Bellow's view of the situation of the artist in contemporary society, the difficulties he faces, and his evaluation of his own potentialities, and approximates a fundamental condition of artistic sensibility which Harold Rosenberg codifies as "the anxiety of art."[29] Rosenberg suggests that "the anxiety of art" is a special insight with metaphysical colouration signifying the uneasiness of art in the face of its own situation. It accompanies an artist's search for identity through various creative strategies and choices, his rejection of shallow or fraudulent solutions, and his reflection upon the role of art among other human activities:

> The anxiety of art is a philosophical quality perceived by artists to be inherent in acts of creation in our time. It manifests itself, first of all, in the questioning of art itself. It places in issue the greatness of the art of the past (How really great was it? How great is it for us?) and the capa-

city of the contemporary spirit to match that greatness...
It is an objective reflection of the indefiniteness of the function of art in present-day society and the possibility of art by newer forms of expression, emotional stimulation, and communication. It relates to the awareness that art today survives in the intersection between the popular media, handicraft, and the applied sciences.... Given the speed and sophistication with which the formal characteristics of new art models are appropriated by the artisans of the commercial media and semi-media (architecture, highway design, etc.), the art object, including masterpieces of the past, exists under constant threat of deformation and loss of identity.[30]

Rosenberg's definition provides a useful speculative matrix for viewing Bellow's artistic problems in perspective and depth. It helps to show how Bellow's struggle with the problem of affirmation, his refusal to consider any separation between the esthetic and moral concerns of art, his view of his own creative process as inspired by a primitive commentator, and his trust in the supremacy of truth in correcting and shaping the designs rendered by the imagination, is centrally related to his anxiety to preserve the sanctity of art, on the one hand, and to liberate it, on the other, from the self-centred or narcissistic sense given to it by the first generation writers of the twentieth-century. Another source of Bellow's anxiety is related to his questioning of the assumption—baldly stated by Lionel Trilling in *Sincerity and Authenticity*—that "the visionary norm of order, peace, honour, and beauty" is out of place in contemporary literature.[31] Trilling points out with considerable intellectual precision that an adherence to this assumption gives rise to a curious dichotomy in contemporary attitudes of life and art:

It would of course be absurd to say that the lives we actually live are controlled by the present-day repudiation of the old visionary norm. As householders, housekeepers, and parents we maintain allegiance to it in practice, possibly even in diffident principle. But as *readers*, as participants in the conscious, formulating part of our life in society, we incline to an antagonistic position. When, for example, a gifted novelist, Saul Bellow, tries through his Moses Herzog to question the prevailing negation of the old vision and to assert the value of the achieved and successful life, we respond with discomfort and embarrassment. And the more, no doubt, because we discern some discomfort and embarrassment on the part of Mr. Bellow himself, arising from his sufficiently accurate apprehension that in controverting the accepted attitude he lays himself open to the terrible charge of philistinism, of being a defector from the ranks of the children of light, a traitor to Spirit.[32]

The truth of Trilling's statement hardly needs to be qualified. It is, however, possible to differ with his use of the word "embarrassment" because the meaning he intends to convey through it is more in the nature of an anxiety to affirm that which is no longer considered worthy of affirmation. The word "embarrassment" implies a certain degree of self-apology concerning one's objectives and strategies. Such an attitude is lacking in Bellow's bold exploration of the possibility of discovering the "visionary norm" in the complex structure of a society uncertain of its aims and hostile to the values cherished by its citizens. Nor is Bellow apologetic about the role he visualises for himself in a cultural situation in which the media competes with the artist and threatens to make him redundant. Bellow is conscious of the difficulties that beset the realisation of the "visionary norm": they contribute in a significant measure to his anxiety, but because they vitally concern his survival as an artist they are in no way a cause of embarrassment. "I see most of my efforts," says Bellow, "as being something in the nature of an experiment, an experiment and a battle. One doesn't necessarily win one's battles. I may be defeated, I may not make it. I don't know that."[33]

Out of the battle that engages Bellow emerges the *raison d'etre* of his art and the celebration of the much ridiculed visionary norm. To chart out Bellow's view of the battle is, therefore, to form a clear conception of his experiment, of the strategies that he has developed to ensure a place for his art in society, and of the nature of the affirmation he regards valid and desirable.

The main issue of the battle, according to Bellow, concerns

certain assumptions about modern society and civilisation that most writers have uncritically accepted as final and used as the basis of their work. The assumptions can be generalised into a theory of distrust in the intrinsic worth of modern society. The theory implies "that modern mass society is frightful, brutal, hostile to whatever is pure in the human spirit, a waste land and a horror. To its ugliness, its bureaucratic regimens, its thefts, its lies, its wars, and its cruelties, the artist can never be reconciled."[34] Bellow's criticism of these assumptions involves neither a defence of the ills of society nor an outright denunciation of the sociological and historical critiques that mourn the decay of modern civilization. He does not brand the critiques as untrue, but he feels that their currency has encouraged an attitude of "unearned bitterness" among writers. By raising such sweeping hypotheses to the level of truth, the modern writer has shied away from the mystery of life and committed his art to opinions of doubtful veracity. Besides, speculations about the whole history of mankind can put the adequacy of any intellectual critique to serious doubt because the subject itself is far too complex to be resolved by any kind of epistemology. A novelist who bases his work on received opinions of "good and evil, justice and injustice, social despair and hope, metaphysical pessimism and ideology" operates under severe constraints and is no better than "others who are involved cognitively with these dilemmas."[35] Opinions are, therefore, inimical to the spirit of art: they can be accepted, questioned, dismissed. A work of art can't be questioned or dismissed."[36]

Bellow's pragmatic view of the prophecies that predict the end of civilisation is related to his belief in the affirmative dimension of literature. "Maybe civilisation *is* dying," he says rhetorically, "but it still exists, and meanwhile we have our choice: we can either rain more blows on it, or try to redeem it."[37] He finds fault with the protagonist of Jean Dutourd's novel *Five A.M.* for being constantly disgusted with life because, to Bellow, man's existence in the vast universe of non-being is, by itself, no small matter.[38] Bellow states the proposition involving life and art in plain and unambiguous terms— "either we want life to continue or we do not." It is needless to write books without a regard for life: "The wish for death is powerful and silent. It respects actions: it has no need of words."[39] The "essence of the moral question," according to Bellow, is: "In what form shall life be justified?"[40] A writer is affirmative and moral "to the degree that his imagination indicates to us how we may answer naturally, without strained arguments, with a spontaneous, mysterious proof that has no need to argue with despair."[41]

Bellow does not, however, avert his face from the problems of modern society. If technology extends the promise of well-being, it also induces a "poverty of the soul as terrible as that of the body."[42] The increase of material comforts blurs the sense of reality of the masses, producing inner vacuum and purposelessness: it levels up individual differences and erodes the variety of life on which the novelist thrives for his selection of suitable subjects. Bellow narrates his disconcerting experience of touring through the state of Illinois in search of material for an article and his discovery that Illinois could not be distinguished from Indiana, Michigan, Iowa, or Missouri.[43] Whether one looked at the houses and their furniture or at the magazines or the hair styles, the salad dressings or the clothes, the choices appeared the same. Bellow feels that modern mass-society has no respect for creative individuality: it forges a system that partly "denatures" the individual by constructing roles for him to deal with various social situations: it sets up standards of propriety and normalcy, "prefers preparedness to impulse," and "resists new forms of reality."[44] Yet, Bellow asserts, it does not suppress human qualities altogether: "they remain private and are mingled with other private things which vex us or of which we feel ashamed. But they are not lost."[45] In Bellow's arresting phrase, they constitute an individual's "sealed treasure."

The task of the writer, Bellow maintains, is to discover and affirm this private treasure *in spite* of the social system that forces "certain elements of the genius of our species to go into hiding."[46] He realises that the search for such missing ingredients is made difficult by a "literary prejudice" about modern notions of virtue and goodness. After the publication of *Herzog*, he confessed in the *Paris Review* interview that he had not represented any really good men in his novels because he did not know who and what they were.[47] Following his attempt to portray a good man in *Mr. Sammler's Planet*, he claimed in his *Chicago Review* interview that intellectual writers could not successfully depict goodness because "Literature in the last hundred years has specialized in being realistic about virtue," making it very hard for writers to "combine intelligence with kindliness."[48] Influenced by the "realistic" attitude to virtue, modern writers have primarily devoted themselves to a rejection of the hypocrisy of the good. Bellow feels that writers should not succumb to such unscrutinized prejudices: they should "in every generation ... look with their own eyes."[49] They should not underestimate the dehumanising character of modern mass-society, but should also not exaggerate its terrors. There is much in modern civilisation that is unbearable, much that offers "good reasons for revulsion and fear."[50] But mere disgust and terror do not account for the whole truth of the world. Since the writer's concern is with truth, he must find "enduring intuitions" to identify "occasions of suffering or occasions of happiness, in spite of all distortion and blearing."[51]

It is such enduring intuitions of life's priorities that Bellow finds wanting in the fiction of his contemporaries. He glances at the work of James Jones, James Baldwin, Philip Roth, John O'Hara, John Updike, and J.P. Donleavy and concludes that the main intention of the writer, whether he adopts the tone of stoicism, nihilistic anger, aestheticism, or comedy, is to show man as completely dwarfed by the pressures of mass-society. Literature constantly bemoans the decay of man's potentialities and exaggerates his despair. Contemporary writers have indicated, says Bellow, "how great our error is, but for the rest they have offered us thin fare."[52] Contemporary literature does not merely discard the conception of the self it considers irrelevant, it vengefully curses it:

> It hates it. It rends it, annihilates it. It would rather have the maddest chaos it can invoke than a conception of life it has found false. But after this destruction, what ?[53]

Bellow agrees that the increase in population and recent advances in science have added to the individual's sense of insignificance. But the contemporary writer misrepresents man's true condition by accepting "a bitterness about existence which is mere fashion."[54] Human beings in modern society are not completely devalued: they are "somewhere between a false greatness and false insignificance,"[55] "not gods, not beasts, but savages of a somewhat damaged but not extinguished nobility."[56] To Bellow, the great question is: "When will we see new and higher forms of individuality, purged of old sicknesses and corrected by a deeper awareness of what all men have in common ?"[57] The writer must perpetually fight for the true projection of man's stature. Unafraid of fashionable prejudices, he must think anew about the mystery of the human condition because "it is evident now that polymorphous sexuality and vehement declarations of alienation are not going to produce great works of art."[58]

The writer must not only struggle to discover the true state of man in the confusion and density of mass-society, he must also struggle desperately to make contact with a populace drugged by the infectious commercialism of the mass-media. Backed by the power of money and catering unabashedly to public taste, the media wield great influence and threaten to seize control of what the writer had earlier believed to be his particular domain. To take an elementary example, the writer's use of psychiatry is neutralised by the movies which preach the commonplaces of morality at the same time as they earn millions. The might of such an all-purpose "spiritual materialism" is only one of the causes of a writer's anxiety. Much worse, he finds that the media—through the movies, the popular magazines, and the television—have entered into competition with him and appropriated the special techniques that the best of the twentieth-century writers were hard put to discover."[59]

The media are responsible for, what Bellow calls, a "consciousness explosion," a paranoiac condition in which the masses are constantly exposed to an artificial need for self-dramatisation. "Art," Bellow feels, "is an element of this new self-consciousness."[60] Sick of ordinariness and craving for ecstatic engagement in exciting and exceptional situations, the public uses "art-tinctured ideas" to mould behaviour. As a result, society tends to acquire the appearance of a large mass-theatre:

> No wonder the boundaries between stage and audience are disappearing and that spectators take off their clothes and

mingle with the actors. What the actors have, the spectators have too. Significance is thus dispersed. What is exemplary, deserving of attention, is shared by thousands and by hundreds of thousands. After all Americans have never been very bookish, and in books they generally sought the usable. Even American intellectuals, from Emerson to Norman O. Brown, preferred marvelous conduct to sedentary culture. Now belles letters are licked: beautiful behaviour wins hands down.[61]

Bellow feels that the crudities perpetuated by the gimmicks of audience participation and private fantasies have produced a superficial sense of creativity which seeks, ultimately, to displace true art from the midst of society. "Modernism is in the hands of demagogues, dunces, and businessmen," he complains, "It belongs to the publicity intellectuals. Because of this, the artist loses the benefit of contact with his modernist predecessors and is deprived of certain impulses and of a certain admirable verve."[62]

The artist's predicament in such a situation is particularly difficult. He detests being reduced to a position where he has to compete with the media, yet, for survival, he is forced to evolve creative strategies to purge his art of the pollution introduced by the mass-media. The artist's anxiety to affirm his art in such a situation, therefore, has vital spiritual and esthetic implications. It necessarily calls for a fresh approach to reality, an approach unencumbered by literary and intellectual prejudices. The art for which Bellow makes a plea is independent of theories, presumes no separation from life, and plays close attention to the complexities of particular cases. It holds life sacred and seeks to communicate its variety, richness, power, and mystery through intuitions that contradict stances of alienation and despair. Bellow believes, with Collingwood, that the artist must be a spokesman of the community because it is through him that the conscience of the community finds utterance. "This account of the artist," says Bellow, "is old, much older than Collingwood, very old, but in modern times this truth, which we all feel, is seldom expressed. . . . Art is the community's medicine for the worst disease of mind, the corruption of consciousness."[63]

It is to the eradication of this corruption, to the endowment of a finer and purer sense of being to man, that Bellow's art is pledged.

CHAPTER 2

Fictional Method

If Bellow's anxiety concerning the problem of affirmation helps to define his conception of the role of the artist in contemporary society, it also contributes significantly to an understanding of his method and accounts for the moral reverberations of his novels. The method Bellow employs to achieve affirmation is, therefore, best approached by outlining the important ways in which his creative anxiety finds expression in his novels. Such a manifestation of anxiety, as evidenced in dramatised fictional situations and encounters, serves an essentially negative function as it takes a skeptical attitude to certain cliché modes of affirmation in order to defend their exclusion from Bellow's own fiction. The esthetic priorities that underscore this process of exclusion and elimination, in their turn, suggest the kind of affirmation Bellow considers valid and provide a rationale for his view of the function of art in human life.

The primary cause of Bellow's creative anxiety, as evidenced in his novels, relates to his desire to avoid any type of affirmation that is incompatible with rational or commonsense conceptions of human nature. Although Bellow concedes that a writer is not necessarily committed to rational judgments in his work,[1] he distrusts affirmative modes that belie an innocent faith in the psychic unity of mankind. The protagonist of *Herzog* recalls in a police station during an interrogation following his involvement in a car accident that "he once believed in the appeal of a direct glance, driving aside differences of position, accident, one human being silently opening his heart to another. The recognition of essence by essence" (*H*, p. 294). That such a belief is out of the realm of practical affairs is not lost on Herzog: "Sweet dreams, those! If he tried looking into his eyes, the sergeant would throw the book at him" (*H, Ibid*). In *Mr. Sammler's Planet*, Bellow uses an incidental conversation between the septuagenarian hero and his grandnephew to expose the "idiocy of orthodox affirmation." The grandnephew's reference to a shooting incident involving a gang of fourteen year old black boys brings to Sammler's mind a scene from *War and Peace*:

> The French General Davout, who was very cruel, who was said, I think, to have torn out a man's whiskers by the roots, was sending people to the firing squad in Moscow, but when Pierre Bezhukov came upto him, they looked into each other's eyes. A human look was exchanged, and Pierre was spared. Tolstoy says you don't kill another human being with whom you have exchanged such a look (*SP*, p. 188).

The grandnephew considers the incident marvellous, but Sammler can only "sympathize with such a desire for such a belief" (*SP*, p. 189). He thinks that "Pierre was exceptionally lucky to catch the eye of his executioner" because such events are unlikely in real life (*SP, Ibid*). Yet, he denies that the idea behind such an event is arbitrary or undesirable. "It is a thing worth praying for," he says, "It's based on the belief that there is the same truth in the heart of every human being, or a splash of God's own spirit, and that this is the richest thing we hare in common. And upto a point I would agree" (*SP, Ibid*).

Bellow shares Sammler's dilemma. He distrusts unrealistic and impossible gestures of transcendence, but his fiction admits the possibility of a belief in what all men have in common. The affirmation he strives to achieve is, as a consequence, modified by the limits of caution and credibility: it assumes the character of a norm whose major emphasis is on the question of being human *in spite of* social tendencies and environmental pressures that dehumanise the individual. Asa Leventhal, Tommy Wilhelm, and Moses Herzog—to think of three Below heroes at random—learn in the course of their *ascesis* that they must confront and accept the fate common to all men. If Leventhal develops a sense of responsibility for a hostile near-stranger with whom he shared no recognisable filiations earlier, Wilhelm is involuntarily drawn to mourn the death of a stranger. Herzog, having decided not to kill his ex-wife's paramour after stealthily observing the man bathing his little daughter, acknowledges that "Man liveth not by self alone, but in his brother's face" (*H*, p. 273). These intuitions are always communicated by Bellow within the realm of the possible. They have a structural and thematic justification and do not appear forced or farfetched.

The intuitions that compel the Bellow hero to surrender the autonomy of the private self and seek meaning in the larger framework of human destiny suggest another related source of Bellow's anxiety. He disapproves of the affirmation of the self through the cult of the ego and creates situations in his novels that raise grave doubts about the validity of such a mode of affirmation. The cult of the ego lays an exaggerated trust in the capacity of the self to gain meaning entirely on its own terms and in separation from others. It gives a false sense of sufficiency to the self and encourages it to assume evasive attitudes to reality. The modern ego presumes, says Bellow, that in order "to maintain its stability, the balance that ensures its safety, it must evade every impulse from within, every offer from without in the interest of self-sufficiency."[2] Haunted by impossible notions of personal glory, the self misconceives the nature of reality—the truly authentic, mundane, reality—and finally loses its sense of proportion and discrimination. In such a state, it even mistakes acts of violence and rashness as proper acts of affirmation. "Some of these explosive modern manifestations," to Bellow, "are exactly proportionate to the degree of poisoned autonomy, ego-centricity, isolation, self-imprisonment that the modern soul experiences."[3] The result is that "We are surrounded by self-invented realities, autonomously administered not by single curious persons here and there but large number of individuals who inhabit crowds of ivory towers."[4]

The moral problem of the writer, Bellow feels, is to find ways to penetrate the barrier that the self builds around itself. If the writer can persuade his readers "that the existence of others is a reality, he can then proceed to higher moral questions, questions of justice, questions of duty, of honour."[5] Bellow's own novels confront this moral problem by bringing his protagonists out of an insulated world of the self into a common world. In *Dangling Man*, Joseph discovers that he "had not done well alone" because "To be pushed upon oneself entirely put the very facts of simple existence in doubt" (*DM*, p. 190). Augie is constantly obsessed with the problem of synthesising "independent fate"—representing the self—and love—implying selflessness. Herzog's crisis is caused by his futile quest for marvellous qualities: his recovery is underpinned by the realisation that "Subjective monstrosity must be overcome, must be corrected by community, by useful duty" (*H*, p 219). Sammler's nobility is due to his acceptance of limits: he has no desire to smash "through the masks of appearances" and is content to participate in life's ordinariness with a civil heart (*SP*, p. 136). Bellow's apathy to the cult of the ego helps to spell out his differences with a writer such as Norman Mailer whose account of the hipster is based on a firm belief in the ability of the self to become authentic through a participation in desperate and dangerous situations. As against the necessity of limits and restraint advocated by Bellow for a normal and sane life, Mailer emphasises "immoderation" as the chief characteristic of the Hip ethic.[6] The hipster shares the paranoia of the psychopath, Mailer asserts, and tries to overturn current norms of civilised behaviour in his quest for orgasm, the ultimate form of ecstasy and self-fulfilment to which he aspires:

> Hip, which would return us to ourselves, at no matter what price in individual violence, is the affirmation of the barbarian, for it requires a primitive passion about human nature to believe that individual acts of violence are always to be preferred to the collective violence of the State; it takes literal faith in the creative possibilities of the human being to envisage acts of violence as the catharsis which prepares growth.[7]

In his commitment to the code of violence and barbarism, the hipster obviously tries to outstep the limits that circumscribe the life of an ordinary human being. If the categories suggested by Schlossberg, a secondary character in *The Victim*, are to be employed, the hipster attempts to exceed his humanity through acts of violence and, in the process, becomes less than human. Readers of Bellow would be provoked by the definition of Hip to recall a few characters in his novels whose incessant search for new and exciting adventures eventually weakens their foothold on reality. Humboldt's failure is hastened by his belief that "If life is not intoxicating, it is nothing" (*HG*, p. 28). Jefferson Forman, who died in an aircrash in the Pacific, was perpetually in search of daring experiences and had discovered, like the hipster, that "there were some ways in which to be human was to be unutterably dismal, and that all his life was given over to avoiding those ways" (*DM*, p. 83). Such a craze for uniqueness and distinction, Bellow believes, results from an "unemployed consciousness" unable to find secure moorings in ordinary life: the individual explores "all other states of being in a diffused state of consciousness, not wishing to be any given thing but instead to become comprehensive, entering and leaving at will" (*SP*, p. 235). The hipster, in Bellow's frame of reference, can, thus, be regarded as an individual whose inner vacuum prompts him to indulge in desperate exercises of self-assertion:

> How terrified the soul must be in this vehemence, how little that is really dear to it it can see in these Sadic exercises. And even there, the Marquis de Sade in his crazy way was an Enlightenment philosophe. Mainly he intended blasphemy. But for those who follow (unaware) his recommended practices, the idea no longer is blasphemy, but rather hygiene, pleasure which is hygiene too, and a charmed and *interesting* life. An *interesting* life is the supreme concept of dullards (*SP*, p. 229).

The essential relationship that Bellow conceives between normalcy and ordinariness can be understood in its proper context through a comparison of his stances and attitudes with those of Sylvia Plath in *The Bell Jar*.[8] Both Bellow and Plath show an identical concern with the problem of retaining sanity—or recovering from threats to normalcy—in a society indifferent to human aspirations; but the full comprehension of the issues implicit in the individual's relationship with society, and of the affirmative options available to him, that is found in Bellow's novels is absent in Plath's account of her protagonist's neurosis. *The Bell Jar* is a thinly veiled autobiographical novel about the mental breakdown of a nineteen year old girl after her brief sojourn in New York. Esther Greenwood's crisis is aggravated by her uneasy realisation that the various options open to her are unsatisfactory because they all demand her participation in life's ordinariness. The idea of marriage as a deal of the future appears repugnant to her because "This seemed a dreary and wasted life for a girl with fifteen years of straight A's."[9] She also rejects the fate of motherhood because "Children made me sick."[10] Her relationship with her mother lacks warmth and borders on feelings of murderous hatred: her mother's snoring, to take a small example, irritates her so much that the only way she can think of stopping it is "to take the column of skin and sinew from which it rose and twist it in silence between my hands."[11] Her artistic ambitions receive a setback after a rebuff from the editor of a ladies' journal who had initially encouraged her with a prize scholarship. She tries her hand at a novel but gives up because she thinks she lacks the basic experience of life necessary for writing fiction: "How could I write about life when I'd never had a love affair or a baby or seen anybody die."[12] The irony is that this thought occurs to her after she has wilfully turned away from the options that could possibly make such experiences available: she misses those fundamental human experiences in fiction that she has discarded as uninteresting and dull in real life. It is, therefore, natural that she sees

> the years of my life spaced along a road in the form of telephone poles, threaded together by wires. I counted one, two, three . . . nineteen telephone poles, and then the wires dangled into space, and try as I would, I couldn't see a single pole beyond the nineteenth.[13]

The frightening image of the telephone wires dangling in empty space symbolises the despair and vacuity that overwhelm Esther Greenwood in the absence of meaningful self-engagement. Unable to communicate with others and constantly obsessed with feelings of paranoiac righteousness, she finally enters the twilight region of consciousness in which lunacy and coherence are inextricably mixed. She considers and puts into practice one strategy of suicide after another with a glee that is almost demoniac in its negation of life, and though the novel closes with a dim possibility of her release from the asylum, the reader is afforded few insights to gauge the extent of her recovery. The accommodation that she may negotiate with her environment in the future appears doubtful because her cure is essentially clinical and not induced by any kind of corrective self-analysis.

The case of Esther Greenwood ought to interest Bellow's readers because the neurosis of some of his protagonists is the outcome of their intolerance to ordinary life. They too contemplate suicide as an alternative to life's problems, but ultimately follow a pattern of recovery that is denied to Esther Greenwood. Wilhelm vainly pursues a career in the movies despite his unfavourable screen-test because he is unwilling to accept a secondary social placement: his crisis may be attributed to his attempt to conceal his real self behind the mask of success. Herzog loses track of his deteriorating domestic life in his intellectual exploration of the basis of marvellous conduct: the result is a second divorce and an incomplete research project ambitiously aimed at correcting the last of the Romantic errors about the self. Wilhelm's sensibility is always flooded by images of self-castigation and death: his recovery seems possible only after his realisation that he is not exceptional or unique but is a part of a large entity that subsumes his and everybody else's strivings. Even in the midst of his acute crisis, Herzog is able to hold in check his thoughts of death by his sense of duty to himself, to his children, to life: "*He* could not allow himself to die yet... His duty was to live. To be sane, and to live, and to look after the kids" (*H*, p. 27). It is important for Charlie Citrine to learn that the ordinary universe cannot be dodged by any of his gimmicks and that, as Herzog discovers, the "strength of a man's virtue or spiritual capacity (must be) measured by his ordinary life" (*H*, p. 106). This explains Sammler's preference for Kierkegaard's Knight of Faith, who "having set its relations with the infinite, was entirely at home in the finite. Able to carry the jewel of faith, making the motions of the infinite, and as a result needing nothing but the finite and the usual" (*SP*, p. 63).

Bellow believes that suicide is a derisive act of revenge by the unemployed self on life, a nihilistic gesture denying that human life by itself is valuable and purposive. The ineluctable fact of death's ultimacy, in his view, should inspire the individual to infuse his life with significance. "The lesson of the dead," he writes in a review of Morris Engel's films, "is that (man) must act before it is too late. He must fulfil himself before he is overtaken by the grave."[14] Haunted perpetually by the desire to do good, Charlie Citrine suffers from the overwhelming need to "capture a true and clear word ... as my human day ended" (*HG*, p. 199). Sammler believes that death is not an opportunity of escape from the rigours of life, but a moment of honour inviting the individual to summon his finest qualities (*SP*, p. 81). The desire to lead a significant life before death, according to Herzog, is the "dream of man's heart" (*H*, p. 303); it is a knowledge innate to the human being, an important pre-condition of the contract that determines his existence on the earth (*SP*, p. 313).

Man's search for significance is often distracted and confused, in Bellow's world, by the tendency of the human mind to attempt intellectual formulations of the nature of life. Bellow considers such "ideal constructions" of reality suspect because they are not motivated by a regard for truth and depend mainly on verbal ingenuity: "You get a fix on some particular explanation," he says, "and you can be struck by the relevance of that explanation to everything that comes along."[15] A writer is primarily concerned with truth and cannot afford to rely on any particular theory of life in his fiction because no theory can ever totally reflect reality. Reality, in Bellow's view, is intractable and multiform, out of the reach of intellection and ratiocination. It is a given that cannot be avoided and has to be accepted in its full mystery and complexity.

Bellow's novels give abundant expression to his anxiety to explore a mode of affirmation independent of theories and explanations. The Bellow hero goes beyond the ideal construction invented by himself or by his Reality Instructors to come to terms with reality and recognise his significance. He learns that all explanations are merly a cluster of ideas—the "plastered idols of the Appearances," in Citrine's phrase (*HG*, p. 16)—unrelated to the natural knowledge of the soul: they are superfluous and lead a man away from himself. Henderson, contemplating the fate of King Dahfu in retrospect, realises that the King lost his life because his theories of improving the human personality had made him oblivious of the world around him:

> ... he had a hunch about the lions; about the human mind; about the imagination, the intelligence, and the future of the human race. Because, you see, intelligence is free now (he said), and it can start anywhere or go anywhere. And it is possible that he lost his head, and that he was carried away by his ideas. This was because he was no mere dreamer but one of those dreamer-doers, a guy with a program. And when I say that he lost his head, what I mean is not that his judgment abandoned him but that his enthusiasms and visions swept him far out (*HRK*, pp. 234-235).

Bellow's distrust of intellection is at times responsible for his near-lyrical celebration of the wonder of existence in its non-intellectual aspects. He contrasts human and other forms of life to suggest that man alone is not satisfied to be what he is and vainly tries to meet the requirements of his own definitions of himself. The following passages from Bellow's story "Mosby's Memoirs" bring into focus the contrast between man's desire to be more than what he is and the contentment of being enjoyed by other creatures:

> Embroidering the trees, the birds of Mexico, looking at Mosby, and the hummingbird, so neat in its lust, vibrating tinily, and the lizard on the soil drinking heat with its belly.[16]
> A most peculiar, ingenious, hungry, aspiring, and heartbroken animal, who by calling himself Man, thinks he can escape being what he really is. Not a matter of his definition, in the last analysis, but of his being. Let him say what he likes.[17]

To Bellow, the presence of human Life in a vast inanimate universe is in itself a matter of considerable satisfaction. The contemplation of the marvels of nature may not bring a sense of security, yet "there is a sweetness in being which may (nevertheless) be tasted."[18] Henderson reads the Biblical description of the lilacs of the field outshining Solomon in all his glory and feels strangely moved and comforted. Herzog, nearing the resolution of his crisis, is happy to leave behind his hectic cerebration and is "pretty well satisfied to be, to be just as it is willed, and for as long as I may remain in occupancy" (*H*, p. 340). Citrine experiences the bliss of being during his flight to New York: "I could find no shadow of wistful yearning, no remorse, no anxiety. I was with a beautiful binn. She was as full of schemes and secrets as the court of Byzantium. Was that so bad ? I was a goofy old chaser. But what of it ?" (*HG*, p. 313).

The sheer joy in existence experienced by the Bellow hero is one aspect of the significance sought by him; another important aspect may be located in his recognition of the need to cultivate "prosocial" attitudes in a society in which mass-behaviour generally tends to be self-directed.[19] Bellow vividly communicates the indifference of the man in the street through an incident recounted by Allbee in *The Victim*. A man in the subway accidentally steps on the tracks and is pinned against the wall by an oncoming train:

> He was bleeding to death. A policeman came down and right away forbid anyone to touch this man until the ambulance arrived. That was because he had instructions about accidents. Now that's too much of one thing—playing it safe. The impulse is to save the man, but the policy is to stick to rules. The ambulance came and the man was dragged out and died right away....
> .... And the crowd! The trains were held up and the station was jammed. They kept coming down. People should have pushed the cop out of the way and taken the fellow down. But everybody stood and listened to him (*TV*, pp. 225-226).

In Bellow's protagonists, the impulse to help, to be good, to respond to the plight of another human being coexists with the purely self-centred impulse to remain uninvolved and impassive. Thus, Joseph, in spite of his marginal, dangling state, speculates on the nature of good life and considers the possibility of establishing a "colony of the spirit" cleansed of spite and rancour. Augie March is obsessed by the idea of an independent fate, but wishes to establish a foster-home. The system of values which Herzog comes to accept includes compassion, togetherness, and duty. Sammler is convinced that the purposive enagement of an individual by other human beings gives depth and direction to life.

Such altruistic aspirations are, however, balanced by Bellow's sensitivity to the excessive and sentimental enthusiasm that often accompanies the desire to do a good deed. He spoofs such impulses and shows that their motives can be suspect and their repercussions painful and sad. Citrine accurately perceives that Humboldt's desire to do good often amounted to a manipulation of others: "Lie there. Hold still. Don't wiggle. My happiness may be peculiar, but once happy I will make you happy... when I am satisfied the blessings of fulfillment will flow to all mankind" (*HG*, p. 23). Henderson, trying to solve the problem of water-pollution in the Arnewi village, blows up the only source of water-supply and has to beat a guilty and shameful retreat. Sammler makes an unsuccessful attempt to report a black pickpocket to an unconcerned police officer and unnecessarily exposes himself to the criminal's threat.

The social-mindedness that has increasingly preoccupied Bellow in his novels may be said to represent his unconscious participation in the general shift toward positive forms of behaviour observed in the American society by behavioural scientistis such as Gouldner, Berkowitz, Campbell, Latane, and Darley. In a special number of *The Journal of Social Issues* devoted to a consideration of prosocial behaviour, Lauren G. Wispe noted:

> The possibility exists that during the past decade some important social psychological theory and research and some salient social forces may have interacted to produce a subtle shift in the *Zeitgeist* from studies concerned with more negative to more prosocial or positive forms of social behavior.[20]

According to Wispe, the behaviour described as positive or prosocial would be

> expected to produce or maintain the physical and psychological well-being and the integrity of the other person(s)

involved. This kind of behavior intends not only the well-being of the other person(s), but also a willingness to share, however briefly, not only the other's end-in-view, but even his pain, frustration, and sorrow.[21]

Bellow's later novels move closer to a system of ethical imperatives that coincides with Wispe's broad definition of prosocial conduct. These imperatives are rooted in the experience of the Bellow hero and emerge as valid alternatives to the states of mind and being characteristic of an intense commitment to the cult of the ego. Herzog accepts joy in existence for an unrelieved obsession with anguish, togetherness and compassion for alienation and indifference, and a sense of duty—to himself, to his children, to life—for the irresponsibility characteristic of self-directed behaviour. As compared to Herzog, Sammler represents a more conscious recognition of these imperatives and a keener awareness of the sources of stability in life. "There will be no end to suffering," he tells Govinda Lal, an Indian biophysicist, "as long as there is no ethical life and everything is poured so barbarously into personal gesture" (*SP*, p. 235). The love for mankind of which Joseph, Leventhal, Wilhelm, Herzog, and Citrine give unmistakable but tentative evidence finds a more assured anchor in Sammler. He is saddened by the dishevelled state of modern society but is unwilling to abandon it for the moon. He affirms life in spite of its manifold contradicitions and exudes a courage of being unknown to other Bellow heroes.

Bellow's novels dramatise sudden moments of illumination and discernment when the kind of love Sammler has for life is felt by other Bellow heroes as well. Joseph, looking out of a third-floor window, is struck by his affinity with the world, society, and the generation to which he belongs. "We were figures in the same plot," he says, "eternally fixed together. . . their existence . . . made mine possible" (*DM*, p. 25). At crucial moments in *The Victim* and *Seize the Day*, Leventhal and Wilhelm experience transitory but powerful intimations of being part of mankind. O.E. Sperling has pointed out in his psychoanalytic study of social-mindedness that such generalised feelings of love and kinship attest an individual's sense of social obligation.[22] In the case of the later Bellow heroes, such feelings do not merely signify desirable social and ethical conduct, but reach over to a dimension of significance which, for want of a more suitable word, may be called religious. The possibilities of religious life are also dimly visualised by the heroes of Bellow's "victim-novels," but are left unexplored because of their unclear insight into their own situation. The acceptance of God, to Joseph, appears "a miserable surrender... born out of disheartenment and chaos; and out of fear" (*DM*, p. 63). Leventhal is left groping, at the end of *The Victim*, for an "idea of who runs things" (*TV*, p. 294). In *Seize the Day*, Wilhelm prays desperately to God for a release from his miserable life. He has intuitions of being related to and entity greater than himself, but till the end of the novella there is little to suggest that his religious feelings have been fully absorbed in his personality. The heroes of Bellow's "adventure-novels" move beyond the "victim-heroes" in their understanding of their situation and their need to find a centre of belief. Augie, aware of his inability to be still, aspires for a state of spiritual repose because he knows that "When striving stops, the truth comes as a gift—bounty, harmony, love, and so forth" (*AM*, p. 514). Confronting the terror of insignificance and nothingness that had goaded his soul to rebel against inauthenticity, Henderson longs to believe in "Something because of whom there is not Nothing" (*HRK*, p. 253).

Bellow's "novels of survival" approach the religious dimension as an incomprehensible frontier of experience against whose ultimacy all human striving has to be judged. "The survivors," like "the victims" and "the adventurers," need to relate themselves to God, but, in addition, they learn to accept life *as it is willed* in spite of its contradictions and oddities. They do not reason with it nor try to conform it to the ideal conceptions invented by their egoes, but discover in it the purpose of their own existence. *Herzog* indicates that the necessary pre-condition of fulfilling God's "*unknowable will*" is to accept it—and Him—without symbols, to realise that everything in the world acquires "intensest significance" if it is divested of the ego (*H*, p. 326). This does not imply that Herzog recommends, or lapses into, an intellectual inertia. He believes that "*the human intellect is one of the great forces of the universe. It can't ramain safely unused*" (*H*, p. 311). His ambitious research project has been abandoned, but he has "*certain things still to do. And without noise, I hope*" because "*Life on this earth can't be simply a picture*" (*H*, p. 326).

Mr. Sammler's Planet and *Humboldt's Gift* underline the conception of religious life toward which Herzog moves. Sammler considers it unfortunate that the question of belief has largely remained a matter of explanations. Since belief is beyond explanations, the "inability to explain is no ground of disbelief" (*SP*, p. 236). The natural knowledge of the soul, the knowledge that commits the soul to seek significance, defines the modalities of belief and ethical conduct. Love, the basic motivation behind all types of prosocial behaviour, is a natural manifestation of the inner order of a soul infused with the "sense of God" (*SP, Ibid*). Charlie Citrine, tired of his egoistical clowning, realises that he "must fix my whole attention on the great and terrible matters that had put me to sleep for decades" (*HG*, p. 194) and "listen in secret to the sound of the truth that God puts into us" (*HG*, p. 477).

The religious view of life latent in Bellow's novels derives from two basic assumptions. Bellow considers it possible for an individual to step into religious life through a self-generated yearning for significance and to approach God through an acceptance of ordinary reality and the norms of ethical conduct. Modern theologians share these assumptions and agree on their credibility in an age noted for the eclipse of belief in all walks of life. Langdon Gilkey believes that in asking questions about his essence, man "enters that region of experience where language about the ultimate becomes useful and intelligible... where God may be known, and also where the meaningful usage of this word can be found."[23] Religious consciousness inheres, according to Nathan A. Scott, Jr., not in a particular system or symbology or a quest for another world, but in the intuition of "the realities of our human world in relation to a region of things where all value and meaning are ultimately grounded."[24] Martin Buber defines faith as "an entrance into reality, an entrance into the *whole* reality, without reduction or curtailment."[25] Gerhard Ebeling also rejects the commonplace notion that faith is "a kind of speculative soaring into transcendence" and insists that

> Faith : . . . determines existence as existence in this world, and thus it is not something alongside all that I do and suffer, hope and experience, but something that is concretely present in all, that is, it determines all my doing and suffering, hoping and experiencing.[26]

The intellectual flavour of Bellow's novels, which results from the fusion of the prosocial, ethical, and religious strands of contemporary thought, deserves notice because it has not so far been fully appreciated by critics. This is not to say that Bellow's critics deny the intellectual interest that his fiction generates, but that they fail to take cognizance of the intellectual method he employs to convey his vision of religious life. To take a representative instance, Maxwell Geismar calls Bellow a "Novelist of the Intellectuals," but he so restricts his use of the term "intellectual" that the early novels are made to appear a derivative of "the social realism school of Dreiser . . . and of such late figures as Ira Wolfert, James T. Farrell, and Nelson Algern."[27] Geismar does not perceive that the "social realism" of Bellow's novels originates not from a Marxist view of history and society —as he would like it to be—but from their absorption, through a process of intellectual osmosis, of some of those modern trends in theology, sociology, and behavioural science that incline toward prosocial conduct. Bellow is not interested in a truncated realism sustained by a commitment to ideological dogma. Nor does he prefer a non-intellectual and non-spiritual view of man that describes him as a creature governed by his material environment. His choice—as evidenced in the whole body of his work—seems to favour a comprehensive and inclusive form of realism that George Woodcock, in his essay on Ignazio Silone, calls "true realism." True realism, Woodcock submits:

> must seek to portray life in a manner that will embrace all its aspects, whether manifested physically, intellectually, or spiritually. It must reveal to the full extent of the writer's knowledge and ability the nature of human development, and the complex unity of natural law by which it is motivated and governed. The writer who endeavours to show in his work such an integrated view of man and of his relationship with the world in which he lives and works, is

truly a realist.[28]

Geismar glosses over the fact that Bellow's anxiety to temper the creative imagination with the sense of truth motivates him to opt for a mode of representation that takes stock of the totality of reality and the entirety of human experience. He arbitrarily invents a matrix of evaluation that relies on paraphrasable content and is unsuitable for an appreciation of the religious tones on which Bellow's later novels end. It is, therefore, not surprising that in a later review of *Herzog*, Geismar is so annoyed by his inability to conform the novel to his matrix that he accuses Bellow of "nastiness" and "spiritual obscenity" and refuses to find in the protagonist's recovery "any sense of understanding, or recognition, or, God forbid, any possible sense of his own personal or moral resposibility."[29] Nathan A. Scott, Jr. is justified in contending in his criticism of Geismar that "social circumstance never defines the ultimate dimension of selfhood in the world of *Augie March* and *Henderson* and *Herzog*: the human individual is in no way shown here to be merely an epiphenomenon of social proces: personality is not imagined in ways that suggest it to be wholly immersed in a social continuum and reaching only towards a social destiny."[30] Instead, Scott proceeds to show how Bellow avoids soft options and "short cuts to ecstasy" to affirm "something like a principle of *sola gratia*."[31] Useful as Scott's estimate is, one wonders why his recognition of the absence of easy alternatives and quick leaps to faith does not enable him to identify the method that Bellow employs to rule out stereotyped modes of affirmation. Scott also fails to perceive that the "ultimate dimension" of Bellow's novels is not conceived in vacuum, but grows out of the ethical imperatives of human behaviour. He is aware of Geismar's error but he too concerns himself almost exclusively with the paraphrasable content of Bellow's novels and devises a technique of interpretation vulnerable to the distortions introduced by slick verbal jugglery. It is true that studies in fiction cannot possibly do without a certain amount of paraphrasing for referential purposes, but in Scott's case the paraphrase invariably takes the form of highly stylised summaries that substitute for the experience of the texts. It is one thing to try to move beyond formalism to overcome the New Critic's "superstition of the word" and quite another to return, in the process, to the kind of impressionistic re-telling for which T.S. Eliot rightly upbraided Arthur Symons in *The Sacred Wood*.[32] By overlooking the subtleties of Bellow's method, Scott arrives at an assessment that is impervious to the method of connoting the religious dimension. Scott's criticism suffers in the bargain because, in the absence of an understanding of the full range of devices that Bellow uses to give perspective to the predicament of his protagonists, the religious quality of his novels in not only imperfectly grasped, but appears more in the nature of a superimposition. One is reminded in this context of the Russian thinker Nicolas Berdyaev whose exegesis of Dostoevski's novels is little more than an illustration of his own philosophy.[33]

A fuller appreciation of Bellow as an "intellectual novelist" is possible if it is perceived that the method he adopts to deal with the crisis of his protagonists is essentially the same as the one employed by intellectuals to analyse and resolve a problem. It is a method recognised in the history of philosophy for its efficacy in correcting fundamental errors of sensibility: its manner is ironic, it is not prescriptive, and it *implies* conclusions with a kind of inevitability, as a logical consequence of the basic premises, with no other valid alternatives than the ones that appear available. In the second volume of *The Story of Civilization*, entitled *The Life of Greece*, Will Durant brings out the scope and disposition of this method as practised by Socrates:

> His method was simple: he called for the definition of a large idea; he examined the definition, usually to reveal its incompleteness, its contradictoriness, or its absurdity; he led on, by question after question, to a fuller and juster definition, which, however, he never gave. Sometimes he proceeded to a general conception, or exposed another by investigating a long series of particular instances, thereby introducing a measure of induction into Greek logic; sometimes, with the famous Socratic irony, he unveiled the ridiculous consequences of the definition or opinion he wished to destroy.[34]

The Socratic method operates on several levels in Bellow's fiction. In a nutshell, it involves either the correction of the error with which the Bellow hero begins or the presentation to the reader of a perspective highlighting the continuance of the hero in error. Dissatisfied with his situation, the hero obsessively struggles with the problem of bridging the gap between his self and reality. In order to come to terms with reality, he considers it necessary to invent ideal constructions or confront the ideal constructions of his Reality Instructors. Unfortunately for him, reality constantly outmatches his formulations: thus, Joseph, Henderson, Herzog, and Citrine are unable, initially, to reconcile themselves to the fact of ordinariness and death, the two most important aspects of reality. Persisting in error and desperately trying to locate a centre of meaning, the hero hungers after an impossible life—of the colony of the spirit or of marvellous conduct—to the point of breakdown and neurosis. The error is corrected when the hero becomes conscious of the futility of shaping his life entirely on theoretical conceptions. He learns to distrust explanations of reality and acknowledges the necessity of finding peace in the finite and the ordinary. An important part of his recovery follows his recognition of the voice of his soul beyond the clutter of ideas and explanations and his realisation that ethical conduct sanctified by a faith in God infuses human life with significance. He is also helped to an awareness of his error through the particular examples of other people (such as Jefferson Forman in *DM* and the Reality Instructors in *AM*, *HRK*, *H*, and *HG*) who are reduced to a pitiable, tragic, or comic state because of identical attitudes. Giving up his utopian quest for an unattainable life, the hero begins to understand his own creatureliness by experiencing the full range of noble and base emotions and drives that go in the making of the baffling entity that is man. This is an essential step in the hero's acceptance of his humanity and prepares him to accept and affirm the existence of others in its full complexity and mystery.

The Socratic method in Bellow's novels performs an ulterior function. The error of the Bellow hero is due to his adoption of overtly intellectual stances about the nature of reality, stances that gradually cut him off from real life by imprisoning him within his own perceptions. The error is revealed to him through the absurd and comic extremes to which his stances ultimately commit him. The intellectual method, thus, celebrates its prowess by subverting itself and leaving as an alternative a system of viable ethical values that offer the promise of a sane and fulfilled life.

An unclear view of the paradox at the base of Bellow's method explains Max F. Schulz's hesitation in placing "possibly the most cerebral novelist of the current scene in the anti-intellectual camp of American fiction."[35] Bellow must be regarded as an "intellectual novelist" because the process which leads his protagonists to arrive at an anti-intellectual state of mind is essentially intellectual. Schulz's hesitation derives from his presumption that the intellectual and the religious person belong to mutually alien worlds. In the case of Bellow, the proximity of the two worlds can be understood in terms of the vital relationship of intellect and intuition in his fiction and his view of art. In fact, the intensive manifolds of his fiction are primarily determined by the inevitability of this relationship, and the conflict and the resolution that issue from it. To take a generalised example, the hero's persistent attempts to intellectualise his problems are thwarted by his involuntary intuitions of the significance he must seek. Ingmar Bergman's account of his creative process analogically supports the synthesis of intellectual and religious attitudes in Bellow's fiction and dispels any misgivings that Schulz's hesitation may arouse:

> I have been asked . . . about the role of religion in my thinking and film making. To me, religious problems are continuously alive. I never cease to concern myself with them; it goes on every hour of every day. Yet this does not take place on the emotional level, but on an intellectual one . . . . The religious problem is an intellectual one to me: the relationship of my mind to my intuition. The result of this conflict is usually some kind of tower of Babel.[36]

Bellow's interest in comedy offers another related area of investigation where the coexistence of intellectual and religious problems can be discerned. The irony implicit in the correction of intellectual misconceptions by intuitions accounts for the comedy of the ego in Bellow's novels. Although comic elements are visible in the ironies that recoil on Joseph, Leventhal, and Wilhelm, it is from *Augie March* onwards that Bellow uses comedy to help his protagonists' return to recovery. He likens the comic sense of life to the spirit of reason and believes that spoofing can convey the sense of truth that is often obscured by high-minded abstractions and formulations.[37] It is possible for moral seriousness to return in literature, he says, once "superfluity and solemn nonsense (have) been laughed and hooted away by the comic spirit."[38] The romantic notion of the self inspires man not only to exaggerate his worth, but also gives rise, in the event of frustration and disappointment, to a "popular orgy of wretchedness." The power of expression and understanding made available to the "grandsons and grand-daughters of laboring illiterates" had "made them able to deplore their civilized condition": "A mighty and universal spirit of grievances long in abeyance, is uttering its first words, releasing what was perhaps to have been expected—the cry that the world is an oppressor, and that existence is absurd."[39] Comedy offers an antidote to the suffering willed by such an egoistical form of despair: it suggests that man cannot lay claims to uniqueness by wallowing in the suffering and wretchedness he has himself created. The comic despair of Walter Bruch, a secondary character in *Mr. Sammler's Planet*, is due to his realisation that even in depravity he is not sufficiently original. Wilhelm's recovery appears possible because of his instinctive knowledge that he is not exceptional in his suffering and shares the general condition of mankind. Herzog triumphs over madness because he learns that suffering cannot be the sole justification of being human.

The efficacy of laughter in achieving the equilibrium of sanity is closely related to its religious potentialities. Bellow agrees with a statement by Hymen Slate that laughter may be regarded as proof of the existence of God.[40] In his frame of reference, impatience with paradoxes and ambiguities is a symptom of neurotic behaviour (*H*, p. 304). In a sane individual, contradictions evoke, not a feeling of existential disquiet, but a sense of wonder at the variety of life. The sane individual is more open to paradoxes because he is aware that truth inheres in a state of mind that admits the possibility of *either* as well as *or*. He is, in effect, in agreement with the idea that existence is "too *funny* to be uncaused."[41] By laughing away incongruities, man affirms the primal cause that is reflected in the mystery of existence and in whom all contradictions, paradoxes, and tensions are relaxed and resolved. No wonder, the incomprehensible nature of the "ultimate dimension" elicits placid, rather than troubled, responses from Herzog and Sammler. To Herzog, *"This is the only way I have to reach out—out where it is incomprehensible, I can only pray toward it. So... Peace!* (*H*, p. 326). Sammler, in Bellow's eloquent phrase, has reached a state of maturity where he really can enjoy the "luxury of non-intimidation by doom" (*SP*, p. 134).

The use of comedy, thus, preserves the openness of Bellow's method and prevents it from lapsing into solipsism and moral obviousness. It is intimately related to his anxiety to avoid sentimental and artificial affirmation, to highlight the aberrations ingrained in the cult of the ego, and to project a vision of religious life upholding the ineluctability of ordinariness and the desirability of prosocial behaviour. By mocking ideal constructions, it stresses the need to respond to, and enter, reality as it is and conveys the wonder and mystery of existence through enduring intuitions of human significance. It is consistent with Bellow's intention to charge the artistic imagination with the power of truth and to reaffirm the role of the artist in a community struggling to arrive at a meaningful comprehension of its aims and values.

CHAPTER 3

The Victims

The world of the victim-hero is the world of the compulsive. In this world, says Henri F. Ellenberger,

> everything has "physiognomic" character: all objects are infected with decomposition and decay. In fact, the patient is fighting not so much against disgusting "things" as against a general background of disgust, a "counter world" of decaying forms and destroying forms and destroying powers which Von Gebsattel calls *anti-eidos*. In the last analysis, this world shows itself as issuing from a specific type of hampering of self-realization.[1]

Joseph, Leventhal, and Wilhelm belong to this world. They are unable to rid themselves of the feeling that they inhabit an oppressive society whose forces run counter to their aspiration for well-being. They are obsessed by thoughts of persecution, death, and madness, and their anxiety for self-preservation insulates them, atleast initially, against all views of reality other than their own. Repelled by ordinary life, they invent evasive formulae to confront its imagined terrors and support their own marginal existence. Reality, however, outmatches all their manoeuvres, forcing them to come out of the barricades they have built around themselves and to accept the fact of belonging to a common world.

Bellow's early story "Two Morning Monologues," published in *Partisan Review* in 1941, may be said to anticipate *Dangling*

Man, *The Victim*, and *Seize the Day* in its treatment of the state of mind typified by the victim-hero. The story articulates, in two different sections, the thoughts of a boy and a gambler in the period of the Great Depression. The two characters represent different attitudes, but can be classified together in their desire to oppose the world through the constructions of the self. The constructions become necessary for them, as in the case of Joseph, Leventhal, and Wilhelm, because they are *convinced* of their victimhood. The boy is introspective and brooding: he would "like to get away" from his unemployed situation, but is prevented from doing so by his "knowledge", private as well as statistical, of himself. This "self-knowledge" brings him the realisation that it is futile to make any gesture of recovery because he is "nearly sunk": "Total it any way, top to bottom, reverse the order, it makes no difference, the sum is always *sunk*."[2] In comparison, the gambler is outgoing and believes that there is "a way through the cracks."[3] Even then, his view of reality is essentially the same as that of the boy: "It turns out the same; mostly sour loss . . . The card is dark, always . . . I'm not fooled about it."[4]

At the heart of the boy's and the gambler's attitudes lurks a smug conviction about the nature of reality that Bellow tries to challenge in his novels. His aim is not to replace one view of reality with another but to imply that reality is multiform and defies the intricate formulations of the human mind. Thus, Joseph is unable to evade ordinariness through his constructions and decides to give up his freedom. Wilhelm learns, through involuntary intimations, that life is not unnecessary and makes a moving gesture of love by weeping for an unknown dead man. *The Victim*, likewise, is a novel about the self's trial, about a man's gradual awakening to the demands of those with whom he shares no recognisable filiations, and his constant efforts at interpreting his responses to the process of being human to which he is subjected.

In the "victim-novels," the first step in the direction of self-discovery is almost always taken, but the final destination of the protagonist's spiritual progress is left to speculation. Thus, in *The Victim*, Leventhal outgrows, to a limited extent, the impassive and recalcitrant elements in his personality. His feelings of guilty escape "and the accompanying sense of infringement" also disappear (*TV*, p. 285). He is aware that genuine suffering may be caused in the absence of a secure social placement; but he considers it wrong to blame it on someone with a place. Such an error, he reasons, derives from a misplaced "conviction or an illusion that at the start of life, and perhaps even before, a promise had been made" (*TV*, pp. 285-286). Comparing such a promise to a theatre-ticket, he wonders why "tickets, mere tickets, be promised if promises were being made" (*TV*, p. 286) because if there are to be promises, they have to be about things more valuable than mere social placement. The silence of the third person narrator as well as the reflector on what the promise really implies shows Leventhal's incomprehension of life's ultimate concerns and Bellow's unwillingness to commit himself to them. This is further confirmed when, at the end of the novel, Leventhal's query about "who runs things ?" (*TV*, p. 294) is left unanswered.

The problem that confronts the protagonist in *The Victim* corresponds precisely to the general and widespread crisis that threatens man today. Uprooted from his racial bearings and unsure of his religious faith, the individual can no longer derive meaning from a social structure that is indifferent to him and suppresses human values. In a world in which the idea of "who runs things" is uncertain, the only course left to men is to come to terms with one another, to accept their particular destiny within the general framework of human destiny, to feel for the plight of those who have been less fortunate in the "egg race" of life, and to become conscious of the sense of profound responsibility that the interdependence of freedom confers upon them.

The affirmation in the three novels is controlled and qualified in proportion to the limitations of the protagonists. While *Dangling Man* may be called an example of the protagonist's defeat and the author's affirmation, *The Victim* and *Seize the Day* give unmistakable evidence of a dim but positive change in the attitudes of their respective protagonists. The affirmation in each case depends on a comprehension of the protagonist's error through a process of self-induced conflict and analysis. This process is communicated in the "victim-novels" *technically* by a skilful manipulation of the first and third person points of view. In *Dangling Man*, the two points of view are united in the larger frame-work of the diary-form: they issue from and are referred to the sensibility of the protagonist, dramatise his impressions of his environment and other characters, and reveal his highly self-conscious state of mind. The third person point of view is employed as an anonymous and omniscient narrator in *The Victim* and works in harmony with the first person point of view which acts as a reflector of the protagonist's internal processes. The controlled use of the two helps to indicate the limits within which Bellow defines his modes of affirmation. A similar strategy dictates the relationship of the narrator and the reflector in *Seize the Day*, with the important difference that the unidentified narrator of *The Victim* appears considerably "humanised" in the novella. The conjugation of the two points of view in the "victim-novels" gives an ironic focus to the predicament of the pratagonists so as to highlight their error and achieve authorial distance and credibility. The affirmation that consequently becomes manifest lacks sentimentality and is tinctured with the sense of truth that Bellow considers vital for the creative imagination.

DANGLING MAN

A reading of *Dangling Man* today is not likely to be so rewarding as it was to readers in 1944 when the novel first appeared. With the advantage of a critical overview one is prone to compare it with Bellow's later novels and find it, as Bellow himself does now, "plaintive" and "querulous," fastidious to the limit of being rigid, and a little too facile on the much discussed issues of alienation and freedom.[1] In the forties, says Frank Kermode, "the intelligence with which the wretched but hard-thinking hero was placed, his eloquent and intellectually respectable introspection, were what won perspective praise. Now . . . it is hard to find in it the vivacity and inventive power one associates with Bellow."[2] The limitations of the novel were, however, not so apparent to reviewers and critics in 1944: Edmund Wilson praised it as "one of the most honest pieces of testimony on the psychology of a whole generation who have grown up during the war,"[3] and a reviewer in *Time*, though calling the hero of the novel "a pharisaical stinker," admitted that the book was "very carefully written."[4] Although it is possible to account for this shift in critical response to the novel in terms of the change of literary taste in American society over the years under various socio-cultural pressures, it is worthwhile to approach the whole issue from the point of view of Bellow's own artistic problems. In his *Paris Review* interview Bellow stated that *Dangling Man* and *The Victim* did not give him a form in which he felt comfortable because of his reliance on a borrowed European idiom and sensibility. This proved repressive:

> —repressive because ... A writer should be able to express himself easily, naturally, copiously in a form which frees his mind, his energies. Why should he hobble himself with formalities? With a borrowed sensibility? With the desire to be "correct"? ... I soon saw that it was simply not in me to be a mandarin ... I fought free because I had to.[5]

In *Augie March* these restraints were to be overthrown. The carefully studied prose was to give way to a more flexible native slang with Yiddish overtones: the mood was to change from seriousness and inhibition to a comic view of suffering. In *Henderson the Rain King* the style of *Augie March* was to be further modified and controlled to suit the exegincies of a different kind of thematic experience. The I—He shifts in *Herzog* and the extended monologues in *Mr. Sammler's Planet* and *Humboldt's Gift* were to become a variation once again on the form of *Dangling Man* because, in the excitement of discovery that accompanied the writing of *Augie March*, "I had just increased my freedom, and like any emancipated plebeian I abused it at once."[6]

Seen, thus, in the context of Bellow's growth as a novelist, a slight undervaluation in the appreciation of *Dangling Man* is possible. In fact, it should be welcome if it proceeds from a mature understanding of Bellow's development as a writer. If, however, it is the result of a sweeping generalisation, as in the case of Robert Gorham Davis, who finds that "the stated themes have not been resolved nor the questions answered,"[7] it should be resisted by a careful analysis of the novel. For the purpose of honest criticism and sensitive appreciation, it is necessary to indicate at this point the limits within which any interpretation of *Dangling Man* must operate: on the one hand, it must take into account the form of the novel, the special problems it poses before the reader, and the manner in which it acts as a strategy of the informing artistic imagination; on the other, the novel must be regarded as a starting point of a fuller study of Bellow's fiction and an introduction to the specific ways in which he defines and qualifies his mode of affirmation from novel to novel.

Being in the form of a journal, recording the day to day incidents in the life of the narrator-protagonist Joseph, *Dangling Man* makes its own demands on the reader. The obvious problem it presents is that of separating the views of the protagonist from those of the author, of judging the extent to which the former can be trusted and of ascertaining the point from where the latter takes over. Then again, the form, by its nature, precludes multiple perspectives on the theme as everything happens within the enclosure of a single consciousness, enhancing, as a consequence, the possibility of ambiguity in meaning and significantly altering the nature of affirmation. The reader is, thus, at a loss to decide whether he can legitimately identify the hero's predicament with the author's worldview, for very often the hero's acknowledgement of failure turns out to be a variant of the novelists ideal fable of affirmation. On the rhetorical plane of the novel, therefore, the problem of *message* must be approached with sensitivity and not just left to the tares of individual judgment. One important method of avoiding the error resulting from highly individual inferences is to refuse autonomy to isolated statements and to consider their implications only within the total context of the novel. This can be done by studying the surrounding nuances— irony and tone, for instance—and seeing if they hold a pointer to the oncoming *finale*. A close reading of the opening paragraph of *Dangling Man* in the light of the novel's ending demonstrates the efficacy of such a technique and helps to contest Robert Gorham Davis's claim that in *Dangling Man* the thematic progression lacks uniformity and cohesion.

The opening paragraph has been generally interpreted as offering Bellow's—and Joseph's—justification of the journal-form and his attack on the Hemingwayism of the forties.[8] In an "era of hardboileddom," the narrator tells us, keeping a diary is unfashionable because the prevalent code of toughness prescribes a strict control on one's nature: "Do you have feelings? There are correct and incorrect ways of indicating them. Do you have an inner life? It is nobody's business but your own. Do you have emotions? Strangle them" (p. 9). As against "close-mouthed straightforwardness," Bellow's hero proposes introspection to keep track of his "inward transactions," and to face boldly the vital questions of the self. Such questions, he holds, are not easily resolved by the hardboiled because "unpracticed in introspection... (they are)... badly equipped to deal with opponents whom they cannot shoot like big game or outdo in daring" (p. 9).

The irony involved in the sense of advantage Joseph presumes over the hardboiled has been overlooked by critics, who, like Chester Eisinger, have been content to say that in "these passages... Bellow is turning away... from an aesthetic of understatement... which was inimical to that treatment of experience which finds it necessary to discover and lay bare, with little restraint, the thoughts and emotions of its subjects."[9] The opening paragraph does not merely emphasise Bellow's repudiation of a highly popular literary mannerism; more significantly, it refers the reader to the irony which later recoils upon Joseph and brings Bellow's underlying mode of affirmation into perspective. The whole point of this irony can be located if the reader directs these questions to Joseph: What is the guarantee that introvertism will necessarily lead to a discovery of the self? Are not the hardboiled and the introvert different facets of the alienated? It is pertinent to ask these questions because they are posed back to the reader at the end of the novel in Joseph's realisation that the "facts of simple existence" are put in doubt when one is "pushed upon oneself entirely" and that he shall have to look for "other means" to fathom the mystery of life (pp. 190-191). With his limited understanding of the problem he was faced with, Joseph should not have expected to reach a conclusion different from the one at which he finally arrived. The seemingly fragmented diary-form may, thus, be regarded as the product of an artistry conscious of its aims. The limitations of the first person narrative are overcome by certain technical devices—irony, situational flashes and remarks, and the Spirit of Alternatives—which are built into the structure of the novel. These devices are employed to provide a double view of the protagonist, to bring out the contradictions inherent in his personality, and, finally, to hint at the novelist's stance. A proper insight into the working of these devices is useful because it indicates the point where the novelist chooses to stand apart from the commitments of his protagonist. Reuben Frank rightly observes that Bellow "vanishes from the area between the reader and Joseph's consciousness, only to be perceived *behind* the latter, too artfully directing that which we take to be a free and spontaneous movement."[10]

To become conscious of Bellow's technique, then, is to become conscious of his theme, for the novelist's intention becomes manifest not as a stance superimposed upon the novel but through the paradoxes governing the protagonist's personality. The paradoxes, in their turn, are revealed through the subtle use of different technical devices. Since Joseph's consciousness is central to the novel, it is valid to approach the theme through an analysis of his view of himself. To himself, Joseph is the *I*, the participant in experience and the source of contemplation, as well as the *he*, an object to be discussed and commented on. This ability to view himself as a separate entity is both releasing and limiting in its range: it brings into perspective not only the two planes on which Joseph lives, but also the crippling inability of the viewer in him to remedy the sickness from which the viewed suffers. The viewer can note the symptoms, but cannot divine the causes and diagnose the ailment. As a participant in experience, Joseph is time-bound and history-ridden. He cannot escape the society in which he is born and the challenge it poses :

Whether I liked it or not, they were my generation, my society, my world. We were figures in the same plot, eternally fixed together. I was aware, also, that their existence, just as it was, made mine possible. And if, as was often said, this part of the century was approaching the nether curve of a cycle, then I, too, would remain on the bottom and there, extinct, merely add my body, my life, to the base of a coming time (p. 25).

THE VICTIMS

As a spectator and a thinker, on the other hand, Joseph would stand no finitude; in fact, he would jump time and space, if possible, and attain, being. Ordinary existence disgusts him, though he considers it a prerogative to answer the vital existential question : "How should a good man live; what ought he to do?" (p. 39). *Dangling Man* is about Joseph's confrontation with this question during the period of waiting which follows his resignation from his job in the American Travel Bureau to respond to the Army's call for induction. He seeks an answer to this question by submitting himself to a painful trial of loneliness and self-scrutiny, discovering in the process that all possible avenues of escape into life—status, ideology, aestheticism, religion, family, and friends—have been barred to him. Being unemployed he has lost his sense of place and security in society. His disillusionment with Marxism derives from his recognition that vital answers cannot be sought in radical political ideologies. The superior world of the imagination, of art and books, which tempted him earlier with its precious esthetic possibilities, now appears inadequate, though it continues to serve well for his artist friend John Pearl who has discovered in it a connexion with "the best part of mankind" (p. 91). His own talent, he feels, "is for being a citizen, or what is today, called, most apologetically, a good man" (p. 91) His quest for a happy citizenry, however, excludes God, since the pre-condition for religious initiation, to him, is a "miserable surrender . . . born out of disheartenment and chaos" (p. 69). He also turns away from his family and friends, rejecting, thus, another source of purposive and cohesive living. From his wife he already feels alienated, though he continues to live with her and be supported by her in his unemployed state. "We no longer confide in each other," he says, ". . . We have friends, but we no longer see them . . . the main bolt that held us together has given way, and so far I have had no incentive to replace it" (p. 12). This distrust of others finds eloquent expression in Joseph's meeting with his ailing father-in-law. Joseph regards his mother-in-law insufferable and asks his father-in-law rather tactlessly how he had managed to tolerate her so long. Old Almstadt's complacent liking for his wife puzzles Joseph, particularly because he knows that it does not result from hypocrisy or passive resignation :

> There was still another possibility to consider, and that was that he was not resigned and that he did not ignore her as he pretended but ... heard and delighted in her, wanted her slovenly, garrulous, foolish, and coy, and took pleasure in enduring her (p. 22).

Implied in old Almstadt's fond acceptance of his wife is an acceptance of others and of life's ordinariness which Joseph does not share. In Bellow's moral framework he is, therefore, found lacking in the determining quality of humanness—the power to love, to believe in the existence of human beings as such.[11] When a friend tells him that he is "all fenced around" (p. 54), Joseph ignores, the remark, mistakenly believing that by withdrawing from the suffocating actuality of life it is possible to arrive at a more refined conception of human existence. What he really longs for is :

> a "colony of the spirit," or a group whose convenants forbade spite, bloodiness, and cruelty ... The world was crude and it was dangerous and, if no measures were taken, existence could indeed become—in Hobbes's phrase, which had long lodged in Joseph's mind—"nasty, brutish, and short." It need not become so if a number of others would combine to defend themselves against danger and crudity (pp. 39-40).

The source of such a programme perhaps resides in Joseph's fascination for the philosophers of the Enlightenment (p. 11). The Enlightenment motto, "dare to know," meaning "trust your knowledge," emphasised that valid ethical norms can be established by man's total reliance on his reason. Joseph fails to see that such an attitude presupposes ideal categories and that in its degenerate forms it can inflate the ego and intensify loneliness.

In his failure to make this necessary distinction, Joseph can be compared with the protagonist of Dostoevski's *Notes from Underground*.[12] Both can theorise efficiently about ideal possibilities, but cannot transform them into existential realities. But important as the parallel is, it is also very essentialt o distinguish between the situations of the two protagonists. To Dostoevski's hero the events have aleady *happened*: the recall of what he calls his "evil memory" is, thus, necessarily tinged with the insights he has gained the course of his trial. Bellow's hero, on the other hand, is in the midst of experience: events are *happening* to him and he is unable to chart his mental growth as perceptively as Dostoevski's hero can. He, therefore, does not realise that in his quest for an intangible world of the spirit as opposed to the tangible, material world of senses and objects, he has ceased to be authentic.

The impossibility of translating his dream of the "colony of the spirit" into reality is brought home to Joseph at the Servatius party. Joseph is revolted by the insults heaped on his drunken and hypnotised hostess Minna Servatius by Abt, an old suitor she had rejected long ago. His own wife gets drunk and has to be helped into the cab. Feeling let down by such an exhibition of human imperfections, Joseph realises that there are many "treasons" that subvert his cherished ideals: "they were a medium, like air, like water; they passed in and out of you, they made themselves your accomplices; nothing was impenetrable to them" (p. 56). He is also conscious that a search for the ideal to the exclusion of everything else is self-defeating because the ideal might never be realised. The craze for the ideal, for the exceptional and the unique, is manifested not merely in a mad pursuit of excellence; it very often leads to a disregard of the human. Joseph suspects that it is the frustration at not becoming "Great in anything he chose" (p. 86) that possibly accounts for Abt's cruelty to Minna. Likewise, Jefferson Forman, who crashed in the Pacific, preferred a life of excitement because he had "In some fashion discovered there were some ways in which to be human was to be unutterably dismal" (p. 83).

That the ordinary and the dismal, the crass and the stubborn—in fact, all that constitutes reality—cannot be avoided, Joseph learns soon. His day-to-day encounters with relatives and friends and even with total strangers force on him the recognition that he too is earthy and common, vulnerable to anger, suspicion and humiliation, often an object of pity. His maid-servant arrogantly smokes in his presence, making him feel that he is of no consequence (p. 25). He flares up when an old communist aquaintance deliberately ignores him in a restaurant (pp. 32-38) and quarrels with his wife when she asks him to cash her pay-cheque, suspecting that she is making him run errands because she supports him (p. 174). Falsely accused of attempted assault by his niece Etta (p. 71), he is struck by her facial resemblance to him and uneasily recalls that the mother of a boyhood friend had once called him Mephistopheles. He felt then that the woman had sensed that he "Concealed something rotten" (p. 77). Joseph is unable to rid himself of the feeling that in his semblance with Etta and Mephistopheles he shares with mankind its evil. Identified, thus, with the sordid aspects of life almost involuntarily, he discovers that there is another ineluctable fact of reality—the fear of death—which he cannot evade. This prevision comes to him when a man collapses in front of him on the road. Psychically disturbed, he finds that a scratch on his forehead, made when his aunt tried to tear him away from the dead body of his mother, has begun to smart. Although in his waking hours Joseph tries to ignore his fear of death, he is unable to control its projection in his dreams. In the first dream, he finds himself on a mission to reclaim a dead man in a chamber cluttered with the victims of a massacre. To his guide Joseph denies any connection with the deceased, murmuring that he "had merely been asked, as an outsider" (p. 120). The guide smiles in complicity, meaning that "It's well to put oneself in the clear in something like that" (p. 120). Actually, Joseph feels uncomfortable in entering into a conspiracy with the guide because the latter's terrifying ancientness and the infantile looks of the dead men in the chamber lead him to infer vaguely that the guide is a personification of death. Ironically, then, the dream implies that in his attempt to evade death, Joseph has only succeeded in making a deal with it. Also hinted in the dream is Joseph's inability to accept the fact that his fate and that of the dead men is identical.

The inescapable truth of mortality dawns upon Joseph in yet another dream. He hears footsteps behind him in a muddy back-lane and, overtaken, finds the swollen face of the man who had collapsed in the street coming toward him, "Until I felt its bristles and a cold pressure of the nose, the lips kissed me on the temple with a laugh and a groan. Blindly I ran . . ." (p. 122). The dream suggests that howsoever strong one's claims to uniqueness, the kiss of death is implanted on every face. The laugh and the groan indicate the irony and suffering involved in the inevitable condition of being human. Joseph, shocked into the knowledge that he is no exception, is sickened by the suddenness and inevitability of death.

> How many forms he takes, the murderer.... The moment is for him to choose. He may come at a climax of satisfaction or of evil; he may come as one comes to repair a radio or a faucet; mutely, or to pass the time of day, play a game of cards; or with no preliminary, colored with horrible anger, reaching out a muffling hand; or, in a mask of calm, hurry you to your last breath, drawn with a stuttering sigh out of his shadow (pp. 122-123).

The insights gained by Joseph in the course of the novel are brought to a focus in his dialogues with the Spirit of Alternatives. Bellow uses these dialogues with a double advantage: they offer the reader an additional view of Joseph's situation, but, more significantly, they help Joseph arrive at the truth about himself through a process of self-analysis very akin to Socratic midwifery. The two other names of the Spirit of Alternatives, "But on the other Hand" and *"Tu As Raison Aussi,"* suggest its ability to tease Joseph into self-comprehension. In his first session with the Spirit, Joseph confesses that though he himself is alienated in many ways, he considers alienation a "fool's plea" because the alienated individual is so much a part and product of the world he sets out to reject that he is *inextricably* implicated in the dialectic of his denial (p. 137). His attempt to denounce the world merely results in his alienation from himself.

In order to bridge the gap between the self and the world, most people invent their own ideal constructions of reality. "I could name hundreds of those ideal constructions," Joseph says, "Each with its assertions and symbols, each finding—in conduct, in God, in art, in money—its particular answer and each proclaiming: 'this is the only possible way to meet chaos' (p. 140)." He acknowledges that living without an ideal construction is difficult because men do need to give themselves "Some exclusive focus, passionate and engulfing" in order to make sense of their lives. But he wonders if the gap between the ideal construction and the world can really be bridged (p. 140). Although Joseph is unable to find an answer to this question, he is convinced that the basic urge behind the invention of all ideal constructions is the same—the desire for "pure freedom."

> We are all drawn toward the same craters of the spirit—to know what we are and what we are for, to know our purpose, to seek grace. And, if the quest is the same, the differences in our personal histories, which hitherto mean so much to us, become of minor importance (p. 154).

The highest ideal construction, according to Joseph, is "the one that unlocks the imprisoning self" (p. 153). Obviously, Joseph is here distinguishing between the "public self" and the "true self" without taking into account the contradiction inherent in his formulation. If the quest of all men is the same and if differences in personal histories are of little value, how far is one justified in conceiving a self—a personal, separated self—which has to be released from the prison of the public self ? And, then, if a personal self is non-existent, where is the need for an ideal construction to liberate it ? Not aware of this dichotomy, Joseph fails to see that his acknowledgement and affirmation of the fate of mankind, in life and death, runs counter to his quest for an autonomous identity that may preserve him "in this flood of death that has carried off so many like me" (p. 167). He is conscious of the duality of his position, but cannot reason it out. "It is appropriate to ask," he tells the Spirit, "whether I have any business withholding myself from the same fate" (p. 167). He grants that war, bacteria, and other destructive agencies have an obliterating power, but he considers it obligatory to "follow my destiny in spite of them" (p. 168). When, however, the Spirit of Alternatives asks him pointedly if he has a separate destiny, Joseph, conscious of his error, grows pale and uneasy. "I'm not ready to answer," he says, "I have nothing to say to that now" (p. 169).

Joseph's uneasiness and confusion derive from his growing feeling that his search for an autonomous self has been futile and that he has not found a satisfactory answer to the problem of designing a "good life." As a result, he is at a loss to make any use of his freedom. He precipitates his draft-call after a quarrel with his neighbour and his landlord, finding it impossible to withstand the unceasing and relentless pressure of the world around him. He feels that loneliness has not helped him in his struggle and hopes to evolve a more accommodating and comprehensive attitude to reality by participating in war and violence, which evoke unexpected responses in men and reveal them in their essential form.

David D. Galloway[13] compares *Dangling Man* with Camus's *The Stranger* at some length and concludes, rightly, that in terms of metaphysical progression *Dangling Man* moves in an inverse direction to that of *The Stranger*. He errs, however, in his observation that "Joseph begins with a stance remarkably similar to that which Meursault is able to strike only in the last moments of his life."[15] This error proceeds from a mistaken interpretation of the responses of the two protagonists to reality. At the end of Camus's novel, Meursault seems to move away from his earlier attitude of boredom and alienation to joy in the intensity of experience. He rejects the Christian promise of salvation in the other world and claims that his justification for living comes from his affirmation of life in the here and now. Meursault can be said to have attained the spontaniety which, to Erich Fromm,[16] is the pre-condition of positive freedom. Joseph is not open to this awareness. He realises its precious quality in the passage he reads from Goethe and in his nostalgic relapse to moments of childhood when he felt he came face to face with reality. At no point in the novel does he really reach out of himself to affirm life as it is. Lacking the spontaniety of freedom but desiring it intensely, he overacts and joins the army, thereby taking the "other course," outlined by Fromm, to overcome his loneliness and insecurity.

The other course open to him is to fall back, to give up his freedom, and to try to overcome his aloneness by eliminating the gap that has arisen between his individual self and the world. The second course never reunites him with the world, in the way he was related to it before he merged as an "individual," for the fact of his separateness cannot be reversed, it is an escape from an unbearable situation which would make life impossible if it were prolonged. This course of escape, therefore, is characterised by its compulsive character, like every escape from threatening panic, it is also characterised by more or less complete surrender of individuality and the integrity of the self. Thus it is not a solution which leads to happiness and positive freedom, it is, in principle, a solution which . . . assuages an unbearable anxiety and makes life possible by avoiding panic; yet it does not solve the underlying problem and is paid for by a kind of life that often consists only of automatic or compulsive activities.[17]

The pattern of Joseph's self-discovery has greater affinity with Antoine Roquentin's in Sartre's *Nausea*.[18] Both the heroes, alienated from themselves and their environment, view their respective situations as observers and hope to find security in the neat roles they construct for themselves to overcome the "nausea" of a meaningless life. Roquentin's former mistress Anny calls these roles "Privileged Situations" and Roquentin feels that to adopt them is to *presume* a whole way of life.

In each privileged situation, there are certain acts which have to be performed, certain attitudes which have to be assumed, certain words which have to be said—and other attitudes, other words are strictly prohibited.[19]

Like Joseph, Roquentin comes to realise that there is no autonomous self to help him in his struggle against "nausea" and that he has no basis upon which to choose: he *is* freedom and "nausea" *is* the condition of life. In his aloneness, he is "condemned to be free".

I am free: I haven't a single reason for living left, all the ones I have tried have given way and I can't imagine any more. I am still quite young. I still have enough strength to start again. But what must I start again ? . . . I am alone in this white street lined with gardens. Alone and free. But this freedom is rather like death.[20]

The conclusion of *Dangling Man*, like that of *Nausea*, can hardly be said to be in positive terms. Like Sartre, Bellow qualifies his affirmation in proportion to the limitations of his hero and makes it more a matter of perspective than of explicit statements and suggestive actions. Though by enlisting himself in the army Joseph does not reach that ideal of positive freedom which Fromm considers indispensable to self-discovery, yet he is spared the predicament of Dostoevski's "Underground Man" who suffers from spite and inertia and delights in degradation for its own sake. Joseph is also saved from creating ideal constructions of reality which give an illusion of meaning and do not allow men to know the truth about themselves. Then there is Joseph's assurance that he would "be a member of the Army, but not a *part* of it" (p. 133), using the period of his service as a "spiritual preparation" for sounding "creation through other means" (p. 191). This is not an altogether hopeless desire because it is accompanied by the recognition that reality cannot be captured through ideal constructions, that "there are no values outside life" (p. 165), and that a belief in an autonomous self to the exclusion of all human relationships is illusory.

SEIZE THE DAY

The predicament of Tommy Wilhelm in *Seize the Day* is brought into perspective by a skilful combination of the third person narrator and the reflector. The combination signifies that the protagonist's actions, details regarding his environment, and, to a limited extent, the reactions of other characters are reported by the third person narrator while the reflector externalizes the thoughts and feelings of the protagonist, and, thus, dramatises his troubled psychic state. The functions of the third person narrator and the reflector are not, however, always easily discernible and, particularly in the later sections of the novella, the novelist's attempt to bring the protagonist's mocking self-consciousness closer to the narrator's view of him results in a progressive blurring of differences. The distinction between the "two voices" is, however, maintained initially because of the novelist's desire to make the reader aware of the gap between Tommy's private and public faces, or—to employ the jargon of Dr. Tamkin whom Tommy is deceived into trusting—his real and pretender souls. The gap is suggested, technically, by a fine variation in tone: the narrator's attitude is generally sympathetic and is in apparent contrast to the reflector's presentation of Tommy's ironic picture of himself. The sympathetic tone is gradually suppressed, yielding place to Tommy's self-mockery. With the developing action of the novella, the narrator's function is limited to reporting details of fact and occasional insights into the attitude of other characters so much so that at many places the third person reporting is suspended in favour of a direct first person rendering (p. 15). Through a subtle manipulation of the narrator and the reflector at the end of the novella, the novelist achieves a necessary distance toward the protagonist's situation so that the cathartic finale may be presented with restricted affirmative implications. This, in effect, lends a kind of dignity, howsoever sad, to the whole narrative.

The opening paragraph of the novella establishes the relationship between the unidentified narrator and the reflector: the narrator's tone is conversational, affable, and mildly polite, imitating the manner of a genial host intent on making a friendly introduction; at the same time the reflector's ironic intrusions show up in parenthetical insertions, asides, and qualifications. The total effect is to underline Tommy's basic insecurity and self-deception:

> When it came to concealing his troubles, Tommy Wilhelm was not less capable than the next fellow. So at least he thought, and there was a certain amount of evidence to back him up. He had once been an actor—no, not quite, an extra—and he knew what acting should be. Also, he was smoking a cigar, and when a man is smoking a cigar, wearing a hat, he has an advantage; it is harder to find out how he feels. He came from the twenty-third floor down to the lobby on the mezzanine to collect his mail before breakfast, and he believed—he hoped—that he looked passably well: doing all right. It was a matter of sheer hope, because there was not much that he could add to his present effort (p. 3).

The irony implicit in Tommy's "present effort" is reiterated and extended in the second paragraph. He is "out of place" among the old inmates of the Hotel Gloriana, where he lives, because he "was used to an active life and liked to go out energetically in the morning" whereas after breakfast the old guests "had nothing to do but wait out the day" (p. 4).

And for several months, because he had no position, he had kept up his morale by rising early: he was shaved and in the lobby by eight o'clock. He bought the paper and some cigars and drank a coca-cola or two before he went in to breakfast with his father. After breakfast—out, out, out to attend to business. The getting out had in itself become the chief business. But he had realized that he could not keep this up much longer, and today he was afraid. He was aware that his routine was about to break up and he sensed that a huge trouble long presaged but till now formless was due. Before evening he'd know (p. 4).

The vigour and determination behind the sentence "After breakfast—out, out, out to attend to business" is exposed by the reflector's deflating confession, "The getting out had in itself become the chief business." The ironic conclusion is that although Tommy asserts his differences from the old men and women among whom he lives, his condition is no better than theirs and that he ill-conceals the crisis which threatens to overwhelm him. As the private threatens to become public, the pretender soul can no longer keep up appearances: "He was wrong to suppose", he realises somewhat later, "that he was more capable than the next fellow when it came to concealing his troubles. They were clearly written out upon his face" (p. 14).

The gap between the real and pretender souls hinted by the conjugation of the narrator and the reflector can be traced to its source through various shifts in the time-scale of the novella. The main action of the narrative is confined to a day, but the movement toward the climax is heightened by several digressions into Tommy's past which constitute a retrospective review of his own life. Through the recapitulation of crucial moments or choices the origins of Tommy's crisis are explored and details that he is most unhappy to confess are involuntarily brought out. One such seminal choice concerns his decision in early youth to become *Tommy* and to cast off the name—Wilky—his father Dr. Adler called him by. The change of name assumed for Wilhelm an existential significance as it symbolised his adolescent longing to become what he was not and was never to be: it was his earliest assertion of freedom, "Adler being in his mind the title of the species, Tommy the freedom of the person. But Wilky was his inescapable self" (p. 25). *Tommy* stood for the impossible success that Hollywood seemed to promise Wilhelm, an illusion that he willed consciously: "Wilhelm had always had a great longing to be Tommy. He had never, however, succeeded in feeling like Tommy, and had always remained Wilky. When he was drunk he reproached himself horribly as Wilky" (p. 25). Bellow suggests that beneath Wilhelm's commitment to Tommy lurks an arrogance of the spirit that deters him from accepting things as they are and, consequently, delays normal, sensible decisions. Wilhelm persists in a career in films even when the screen-test proves disappointing and invents several intricate versions of the story of his failure—"first boastfully and then out of charity to himself" (p. 15). Later, he resigns his job as a salesman with the Rojax Corporation because the firm wanted a son-in-law to share his territory, a disgrace Tommy would not allow Wilhelm to suffer. In his false idealism, he does not seek an exemption from the war as a family man and leaves his wife to depend on his father (p. 54). Even when he realises that his change of name has been an error as it triggered a chain of ruinous events, his pride prevents him from accepting full responsibility for his actions. With his characteristic irony Bellow makes Wilhelm take shelter behind a metaphysical quibble in order to rationalise his error: "Yes, it had been a stupid thing to do, but it was his imperfect judgment at the age of twenty which should be blamed" (p. 25).

The crucial *but* in the clumsy quibble points to an aspect of Wilhelm's personality that is closely related to his vanity: his wilful evasion of reality and his infantile and immature way of dealing with life's problems. This attitude can be interpreted, at one level, in terms of the foolish starts Wilhelm has made in his career and his feeble attempts to defend and explain them somehow. At an inter-related but more complex psychological level, however, it is possible to regard Wilhelm's immaturity as a function of his latent inability to confront the problems of adulthood and his compulsive regression to the reflexes of a sulking child. Deep within he has been Wilky, the abused child, or Velvel, his grandfather's dear, dominated forever by Tommy, his pretender soul, and Dr. Adler, his father, who always seemed aloof, correct, and prim. Nervous and brooding, Wilhelm constantly needs stimulants and sedatives to keep himself in order. Dr. Adler is puzzled by his nervous reflexes: "Why the devil can't he stand still when we're talking? He's either hoisting his pants up and down by the pockets or jittering with his feet. A regular mountain of tics he is getting to be" (pp. 27-28). These physiological manifestations of Wilhelm's infantalism derive from his basic insecurity, his hunger for love, and his great need to reach over to some centre of belief and trust. His relationship with his father and Dr. Tamkin, who eventually cheats him, has to be viewed in the wider context of these personality-problems.

Bellow contrives a variety of intricate emotional equations to express the bond of attachment and resentment Wilhelm has with his father. Wilhelm's defiance of Dr. Adler, symbolically culminating in his change of name, in no way subtracts from his innate desire to receive help and advice from the old man, despite the latter's precise and deliberately half-blind way of categorising his son's problems in pre-defined slots of true and false, right and wrong, genuine and fake. "You make too much of your problems," his father tells him, "They ought not to be turned into a career. Concentrate on real troubles—fatal sickness, accidents" (p. 45). When refused financial help, Wilhelm grumbles against his father's selfishness, but money is not all he wants. It is his craving for sympathy that seeks satiation. "It isn't the money," he tells himself, "but only the assistance: not even assistance, but just the feeling" (p. 56). Bellow offers stray hints in the novella to create the impression that Wilhelm considers his own existence compulsively tied to his father's, so much so that one makes the other possible. His father's acute consciousness of oncoming old age and death is, as a result, a potential source of psychotic disturbance to Wilhelm because he senses in it the tidings of his own end. He tells Tamkin:

"My father's death blots out all other considerations from his mind. He forces me to think about it, too. Then he hates me because he succeeds. When I get desperate—of course I think about money. But I don't want anything to happen to him. I certainly don't want him to die . . . "
"You love your old man ?"
Wilhelm gasped at this. "Of course, of course, I love him. My father, My mother—" As he said this there was a great pull at the very center of his soul. When a fish strikes the line you feel the live force in your hand. A mysterious being beneath the water, driven by hunger, has taken the hook and rushes away and fights, writhing. Wilhelm never identified what struck within him. It did not reveal itself. It got away (pp. 92-93).

Wilhelm turns to Tamkin in his search for the satisfaction he finds wanting in his relationship with his father. In this sense, at least, Tamkin may be called his surrogate-father. Also, Tamkin's unbelievable tales of self-glorification represent a fulfilment of Wilhelm's own unrealised fantasies. Glib and somewhat paranoiac, Tamkin is a typical Bellow Reality Instructor, with his own ingenious formulae to meet the chaos of life. Wilhem is not always fooled by Tamkin's stories, but his need to believe is so great that even the strongest suspicions will not make him walk out on the man. Besides, the investment Tamkin has made for him in the stock-market is his last hope of financial and—connectedly—emotional recovery: he must, therefore, will himself to trust one whose business is to dupe the gullible. Like Allbee in *The Victim* and Valentine Gersbach in *Herzog*, Tamkin is the ambiguous entity deliberately left undefined in the novella. Wilhelm, in spite of his bitterness and resentment, is unable to make up his mind about him till the end. The mystery surrounding Tamkin's personality has, in truth, a revelatory function since in relation to it Wilhelm's own psychic map is charted out and his intense concern with his identity brought into a focus. Also, in an attempt to qualify his affirmation in *Seize the Day* and retain an attitude of ambivalence toward Wilhelm's bid for self-recovery, Bellow puts the right clues for his protagonist—clues which relate to his anxiety to find himself and ultimately motivate his transcendence—in the mouth of Tamkin who employs them to establish his credentials and to pursue his own advantage. Tamkin wraps these clues in psychoanalytical jargon, but they are, in essence, religious. One suspects that Bellow's aim in making Tamkin the mouthpiece of these clues is to suggest the extent to which truths basic to men in all times have been secularised, corrupted through commercialization, and given brand names in contemporary society. Tamkin is an appropriate symbol of this perversion: he trades in these secular cures of the soul just as efficiently as he trades in ingenious methods of amassing riches in the stock-market.

The clue that stirs Wilhelm profoundly concerns the distinction that Tamkin makes between the real and pretender souls, a distinction Wilhem concedes to be true because it accurately mirrors the nature of his own conflict (p. 72). In Tamkin's discourse, the distinction is developed through three progressive, interdependent stages:

1. *The two main souls :* "In here, the human bosom—mine, your's, everybody's—there isn't just one soul. There's a lot of souls. But there are two main ones, the real soul and a pretender soul" (p. 70).
2. (a) *Pretender soul :* "What are thou ?" Nothing. That's the answer. Nothing. In the heart of hearts—nothing ! So of course you can't stand that and want to be something, and you try. But instead of being this something, the man puts it over on everybody instead. You love a little... or give some money to a charity drive. Now that isn't love, is it ? What is it ? Egotism, pure and simple. It's a way to love the pretender soul. Vanity. Only vanity, is what it is. And social control. The interest of the pretender soul is the same as the interest of the social life, the society mechanism" (p. 70).
   (b) *Real Soul :* "The true soul loves the truth" (p. 71).
3. *Conflict between the two souls :* (a) "... the pretender soul takes away the energy of the true soul and makes it feeble, like a parasite. It happens unconsiously, unawaringly, in the depths of the organism" (p. 71).
   (b) "The real soul is the one that pays the price. It suffers and gets sick, and it realizes that the pretender can't be loved. Because the pretender is a lie... And

when the true soul feels like this, it wants to kill the pretender. The love has turned into hate. Then you become dangerous. A killer. You have to kill the deceiver" (p. 71).

Misinterpreting Tamkin's reference to the true soul's wish to kill the deceiver soul, Wilhelm wonders if he has such aggressive tendencies since, in his own eyes, he has always been a victim. "I don't feel like a murderer," he tells Tamkin, "It's the others who get me. You know—make me feel oppressed" (p. 73). He does not realise that Tamkin is mainly hinting at the self-destructive inclinations that germinate in an individual as an outcome of self-deception; thus, Wilhelm is aware of his victimhood but is unable to diagnose his own masochistic drives. Wilhelm's masochism originates from his unconscious desire to see the pretender soul outdone in some way because it has sapped the vitality of his real soul. In his faulty understanding, the vindication and triumph of the real soul is, thus, related to a morbid commitment to suffering and failure; it is, in effect, a version of the pride that made him continue in wrong choices in early youth. Dr. Adler rightly complains of his habit of making an "opera" of his problems, and Tamkin advises him not to "marry suffering." The fragments of verse that naturally come to his mind celebrate sorrow: "come then sorrow/sweetest sorrow!" (p. 89). He allows himself to be squeezed dry of his little money by his estranged wife, knowing that "no court would have awarded her the amounts he paid" (p. 29). In a bid to dramatise his plight before his father, Wilhelm tries to choke himself (p. 48). He constantly castigates himself for his clumsiness: "Ass! Idiot! Wild Boar! Dumb Mule! Slave! Lousy, wallowing hippopotamus" (p. 55). Bellow vivifies Wilhelm's view of his exploitation by others in the striking image of the Brahma bull being devoured by the piranha fish:

"When I have the money they eat me alive, like those piranha fish in the movie about the Brazilian jungle. It was hideous when they ate up that Brahma bull in the river. He turned pale, just like clay, and in five minutes nothing was left except the skeleton still in one piece, floating away.

When I haven't got it any more, at least they'll let me alone" (p. 76).

Critics such as Daniel Weiss'[1] and John J. Clayton[2] have attempted a psychoanalytic study of Wilhelm's personality largely on the basis of his masochistic traits. Their criticism is useful in parts, but is unfortunately limited by their application of masochism as a very broad and inclusive matrix.[3] While masochism does explain Wilhelm's obsessive compulsive behaviour, it is essentially an element of his total personality-complex, co-existing with other, no less important, traits which fall out of its territory and finally suggest the possibility of his recovery. The emphasis laid by Weiss and Clayton on masochism, to the exclusion of such traits, results in a misinterpretation of certain vital passages in the text and calls for a difference of opinion.

One such passage in question, quoted and commented on by both Clayton and Weiss, occurs at the start of Section IV in the novella, immediately after Wilhelm has been refused help by his father. He is tense, hurt, and angry, smelling the "salt odor of tears in his nose." The full passage, consisting of five sentences, reads as follows:

> But at the same time, since there were depths in Wilhelm not unsuspected by himself, he received a suggestion from some remote element in his thoughts that the business of life, the real business—to carry his peculiar burden, to feel shame and impotency, to taste these quelled tears—the only important business, the highest business was being done. Maybe the making of mistakes expressed the very purpose of his life and the essence of his being here. Maybe he was supposed to make them and suffer from them on this earth. And though he had raised himself above Mr. Perls and his father because they adored money, still they were called to act energetically and this was better than to yell and cry, pray and beg, poke and blunder and go by fits and starts and fall upon the thorns of life. And finally sink beneath that watery floor—would that be tough luck, or would it be good riddance (p. 56).

Weiss quotes just the first three sentences from the passage, Clayton the first two. Weiss takes the passage to imply Wilhelm's "despair," "resignation," and "neurotic fatalism,"[4] Clayton asserts that it contains a "summation" of the "life of a moral masochist."[5] Clayton treats the passage in a vacuum. without referring it to its context. Weiss, on the other hand, supplies to it a context that it does not really have: at least two events mentioned by him—the debacle in the stock-exchange and Tamkin's disappearance—have not taken place when Wilhelm is struck by the meaning of his shame and helplessness. Moreover, the two critics also do not analyse the entire passage and ignore, in the process, the qualifiers that Bellow employs to modify and restrict the rhetorical impact of Wilhelm's conflict. A close scrutiny of the passage, in the light of its immediate and related contexts, is helpful not only to show where Weiss and Clayton have erred, but also to chart out the course of Wilhelm's recovery.

The passage has, as its referent, two contexts. The immediate context is, of course, Wilhelm's disappointment with his father's indifference, but the mention of his "peculiar burden" points to another, related, passage and makes explicit the meaning toward which he gropes. The two passages are on the same time-scale: the first (quoted earlier) occurs at the *end* of Wilhelm's breakfast session with his father and Mr. Perls, a co-resident in the Gloriana; the second forms part of Wilhelm's realisation *during* the breakfast that his father is trying to increase Mr. Perls' respect for him by making complimentary, though superficial, references to him. He wonders if the truth about him can be concealed this way and if the purpose of a man's life is not to carry his characteristic self:

The spirit, the peculiar burden of his existence lay upon him like an accretion, a load, a hump. In any moment of quiet, when sheer fatigue prevented him from struggling, he was apt to feel this mysterious weight, this growth or collection of nameless things which it was the business of his life to carry about. This must be what a man was for ... this Wilky, or Tommy Wilhelm, forty-four years old, father of two sons, at present living in the Hotal Gloriana, was assigned to be the carrier of a load which was his own self, his characteristic self. There was no figure or estimate for the value of this load. But it is probably exaggerated by the subject, T.W. Who is a visionary sort of animal. Who has to believe that he can know why he exists. Though he has never seriously tried to find out why (pp. 38-39).

Through the consciousness of Wilhelm, "Who is a visionary sort of animal. Who has to believe why he exists" (p. 39), Bellow, in this passage, appears to hint at his view of man. A man, after all, is what he is in the finally absurd sense, but it is his visionary quality that distinguishes him and teases him to probe the secret of his essence. An intense awareness of one's real being—the paradoxes of one's nature, one's strengths and limitations, fears and hopes—constitutes, for Bellow, authentic human existence. The irony is that men suppress the awareness of what they really are by imposing upon themselves constructions of make-belief, of what they are not but would wish to be. It is, therefore, only in "a moment of quiet," when struggles have ceased and the pretensions dropped, that the closeness of the mysterious soul is felt. The "peculiar burden," which men realise is the business of their lives to carry about, is that of the soul.

These ideas are amplified and related to Wilhelm's conflict in the passage that Weiss and Clayton erroneously regard as a confession of masochism. This would be obvious if the rhetorical structure of the passage is analysed. What is simply referred to as Wilhelm's "business of life" in the related passage (p. 39), is here underscored by three progressively emphatic adjectives—"the real business," "the only important business," and "the highest business." Wilhelm's "peculiar burden" is also defined as the capacity "to feel shame and impotence, to taste these quelled tears." The narrator's parenthetic comment that "there were depths in Wilhelm not unsuspected by himself" should be taken in conjunction with the earlier passage to imply Wilhelm's potential to confront the problem of his identity, and his awareness, howsoever dim, of this potential. Bellow does not confirm or question Wilhelm's views in this passage; beyond the parenthetic remark about "depths in Wilhelm," the voice of the narrator is kept subdued and provides no external clue to the errors embedded in the protagonist's self-analysis. This is done perhaps to restrict any possible speculation on the nature of the oncoming climax. The use of qualifiers ("Maybe" and the interrogative mark at the end of the passage) lends an uncertain, hesitant, tentative, and exploratory quality to Wilhelm's self-search. Since he is always obsessed by his own victimhood, he is anxious to know if giving expression to his true soul, his habit of making wrong choices and suffering from them, is not a sign of authenticity. He compares his suffering predicament with that of his father and Mr. Perls, wondering if their energy puts them at an advantage over him.

In truth, however, Wilhelm's assumptions is wrong because in Bellow's view of life neither the repressed nor the energetic escape the "craters of the spirit" to which they are subjected by their instinctive desire to throw away the vain constructions imposed on the soul. In this respect, Bellow's introverts—Joseph, Leventhal, Wilhelm, Herzog, Sammler, and Citrine—share the same anguish and uncertainty that haunts his extroverts—Augie and Henderson—who are temperamentally more boisterous and open to life. Wilhelm is so overwhelmed by his supposed disadvantage in being less energetic and, consequently, more vulnerable that he overlooks his own oft-repeated complaint about his father's constant fear of death (pp. 92-93). The final question that he addresses himself concerns, quite logically, his attitude to death. Bellow leaves the question suspended between two possible alternatives— "tough luck" and "good riddance" —without committing Wilhelm to any specific answer. Still, the alternatives in themselves are not without an affirmative dimension because they coalesce with a stance fundamental to Bellow's view of the moral function of writing. "Not many people will disagree," says Bellow, "if the proposition is put as follows—either we want life to continue or we do not. If we don't want to continue, why write books ? The wish for death is powerful and silent. It respects actions; it has no need of words."[6] The "essence of the moral question" is not contained, for Bellow, in the rhetoric of death-wish, but in the manner in which a writer chooses to justify life. "We call a writer to be moral to the degree that his imagination indicates to us how we may answer naturally, without strained arguments, with a spontaneous mysterious proof that has no need to argue with despair."[7] For Wilhelm, the poser—"tough luck" or "good riddance"—is crucial because it seeks to determine how precious life is for him: if life is without meaning, death should be "good riddance," but if it has some meaning, it would be "tough luck" to die.

In a controlled sense, therefore, the passage cited as an illustration of Wilhelm's masochism may be said to affirm his potentialities in three possible ways: it projects his intense desire to discover and lead an authentic life; it cancels out, by implication, any disadvantage he might suffer because of his victimhood, and brings his lot closer to that of other Bellow heroes and all men; and finally, by confronting him with the fact of death, it makes him grapple with the problem of meaning in life. Bellow's aim seems to be to hint at the marginal possibilities of recovery that persist in Wilhelm in spite of his virtually chronic sense of failure and oppression. Strewn in the novella are several instances of intuitive cognition which stress his possibilities and suggest that death may not, after all, be a "good riddance" for him. Early in the novella, Bellow negatively locates Wilhelm's need to believe in his strong dislike of cynicism and falsity:

> ... was he also, in his heart, cynical ? So many people nowadays were. No one seemed satisfied, and Wilhelm was especially horrified by the cynicism of successful people. Cynicism was bread and meat to everyone (pp. 16-17).

The negative suggestion acquires positive overtones in Wilhelm's humble prayer to God. He asks for a release from the suffocating prison of his thoughts and troubles and seeks forgiveness and a new life (p. 26). His craving for mercy is reiterated again in his conversation with Dr. Tamkin who believes that a vicious cycle of aggression is generated by the lust for money: "*M*oney and *M*urder both begin with *M*. *M*achinery. *M*ischief" (p. 69). Responding to the letter through random mental-association, Wilhelm asks: "What about *M*ercy ? *M*ilk-of-human-kindness ?" (*Ibid.*).

Wilhelm's abhorrence of cynicism and his prayer constitute one aspect of his quest for an authentic existence: another important aspect of it is his exposure to contradictory impressions of reality and his acceptance of their validity. The pressures of life in New York cause in him the awareness of a prevasive breakdown of communication between people, their increasing isolation from one another, and the loss of warmth and intensity in filial relationships. Wilhelm realises that an individual's reliance on a private "language," on the notion of his uniqueness, is largely responsible for his inability to relate to others: "Every other man spoke a language entirely his own, which he had figure out by private thinking; he had his own ideas and peculiar ways" (p. 83). Lacking the intellectual apparatus to apply this diagnosis to himself, Wilhelm fails to perceive that his obsession with his role as victim accounts for much of his anguish. Still, he instinctively rejects the glorification of privacy and exclusivness through a transitory but spontaneous intuition that offers him insights beyond individual differences and affirms his bond with all men. In the transcendent realm of this intuition, being an outcast is "one of the small matters" because there is a "larger body" from which "you cannot be separated" (p. 84): "There," Wilhelm feels, "truth for everybody may be found, and confusion is only— only temporary . . ." (*Ibid*.). An "onrush of loving kindness" seizes him when he is struck by the thought that he belongs to an entity greater than himself :

> He loved them. One and all, he passionately loved them. They were his brothers and his sisters. He was imperfect and disfigured himself but what difference did that make if he was united with them by this blaze of love ? And as he walked he began to say, "Oh my brothers—my brothers and my sisters," blessing them all as well as himself (pp. 84-85).

It would obviously be rash to read in Wilhelm's momentary illumination a complete statement of Bellow's belief in the value of intuitive transcendence as a possible and valid mode of affirmation. Bellow's ambivalence can be seen, for that mat er, in the reservations Wilhelm develops regarding the full value of his "involuntary feelings": "What did it come to ?" he asks himself, rationalising his feeling as "another one of those subway things" (p. 85). Nevertheless, his recognition of his affinity with all men, despite the alienation and despair that obtain in modern society, seems to assert an incontrovertible paradox of human existence: man is alone but is also a part of an entity greater than himself; he is finite and earthbound, but also capable, howsoever feebly, of transcendence. Wilhelm's dim comprehension of the paradox inherent in the human condition suggests in a limited sense, his capacity to overcome his neurosis, neurosis being definable, in Bellow's frame of reference, as "the inability to tolerate ambiguous situations" (*H.* p. 370). Wilhelm may not be perfectly at ease with the ambiguity of human existence, but he does not struggle against it and even suspects that it may be his "right clue": "That's the right clue and may do me the most good. Something very big. Truth, like" (p. 85).

Wilhelm's potentiality for transcendence and recovery can also be traced in his longing for serenity and peace. The peace for which he hungers has a transcendental quality because it exists *in spite* of problems and is relaxed in uncertainties. Wilhelm nostalgically recalls his idyllic moments of repose when he was still in employment, forgetting "that that time had had its troubles too" (p. 43). Life in New York has diminished, though not entirely destroyed, his capacity to recapture his cherished moments of peace. The brief mental relief he gets from Tamkin's assurance that "Lard will go back to last year's levels" (p. 81) helps him return to the relaxed state he had once known:

> He breathed in the sugar of the pure morning. He heard the long phrases of the birds. No enemy wanted his life (p. 82).

Weiss's and Clayton's inability to reconcile their view of Wilhelm's masochism with his innate capacity for recovery and transcendence leads them to commit mutually conflicting errors, particularly in their interpretation of the climax of the novella. To Weiss, the climax is a logical extension of Wilhelm's self-suffering attitudes and signifies his total absorption in the role of victim.[8] Clayton, on the other hand, portrays Wilhelm as a confirmed masochist, but, while dealing with the climax, concludes that Weiss exaggerates Wilhelm's victimhood. It may be argued against both the critics that they treat Wilhelm not as a human being but as a perfect representation of a psychotic type. They, therefore, fail to provide a necessary connexion between Wilhelm's character and his fate at the climactic moment of the novella. Weiss misconstrues the meaning of the climax to synchronize it with his version of Wilhelm's personality; in Clayton's case the link between Wilhelm's character and his recovery appears forced because he uses masochism when it suits him and drops it when it doesn't.

The cathartic finale of the novella, which describes Wilhelm mourning the death of a stranger, is as unexpected for the reader as it is for Wilhelm himself. It is, however, not patched on the novella and develops organically from the sequence of events immediately preceding it. More important, it is consistent with Wilhelm's character. Before the climax is introduced, Bellow exposes Wilhelm to a series of frustrating experiences, each plunging him deeper into despair : his money is lost in the stock-market, Tamkin disappears, his father refuses to help, and his estranged wife relentlessly makes more demands on him. The defences which armoured him earlier, thus, gradually crumble. The exhaustion of Wilhelm's pretensions is suggested by his violent reflexes in the telephone-booth when he discovers that he has nothing material to rely on: "He ground his teeth and seized the black box with insane digging fingers and made a stifled cry and pulled" (p. 114). Approximating the reactions of a cornered animal, this image provides a marked contrast to Wilhelm's attempt, at the start of the novella, to use a cigar to shield his real feelings. Bellow juxtaposes his dramatisation of Wilhelm's despair with the image of the great crowd on Broadway :

> And the great, great crowd, the inexhaustible current of millions of every race and kind pouring out, pressing round, of every age, of every genius, possessors of every human secret, antique and future, in every face the refinement of one particular motive or essence—*I labor, I spend, I strive, I design, I love, I cling, I uphold, I give way, I envy, I long, I scorn, I die, I hide, I want.* Faster much faster than any man could make the tally (p. 115).

Rendered in the third person, this passage is reminiscent of an earlier passage in the novella describing Wilhelm's kinship with all men (pp. 84-85). By suppressing the voice of the reflector, Bellow succeeds in understanding the connections between the two passages. Wilhelm has, therefore, no inkling at this time of being a part of a large body and is shown oblivious of the direction he is taking. In spite of these in-built checks and balances, the passage seeks to negate, through indirect inference, the burden of Wilhelm's problems by implying that they are not unique as they are shared by all men. This passage can, thus, be considered an excellent example of the ironic gap between the authors's intended affirmation and the protagonist's limited knowledge.

Pushed into the chapel by the surging crowd, Wilhelm becomes a witness to a funeral. Bellow describes Wilhelm watching the dead man in the coffin in terms of three roughly corresponding physiological and mental stages. Crying "at first softly and from sentiment," he is moved by pity for a fellow-being: "A man—another human creature, was what first went through his thoughts" (p. 117). Then, sobbing aloud from "deeper feelings," he thinks of his own desperate plight: "What'll I do ? I'm stripped and kicked out" (p. 117). Soon, however, he reaches a more profound state of body and mind, "past words, past reason, coherence" (p. 117), beyond the constructions that had kept his true soul in shackles. The confrontation with death, the ultimate frontier of human experience, springs open the "source of all tears" within him: "The great knot of ill and grief in his throat swelled upward and he gave in utterly and held his face and wept" (p. 118). Bellow employs the remarks of other mourners to emphasise the intensity of Wilhelm's feelings and to convey a moving sense of his catharsis: the narrative is denuded of extraneous commentation so that full authorial control is felt and all superfluous straining after effect is avoided.

What Wilhelm sees in the coffin—the image of his father, as Weiss insists,[10] or that of his own pretender soul, as Clayton maintain[11]—is perhaps immaterial. Even if no symbolic representation of any personified figure is seen in the dead man, the meaning of the climax doesn't substantially change. After all, it is Wilhelm's humanity that is ultimately touched—revealing for the first time his mysterious substratum, his real soul, and giving it a silent but eloquent expression: "He ... sank deeper than sorrow, through torn sobs and cries toward the consummation of his heart's ultimate need" (p. 118). Such a consummation radically minimises his obsession with his own problems, enabling him to face life in the raw, without soft options. His worldly problems remain what they are, but he seems to move into a sphere where he has no need to invent deceptions to bolster his vanity. Having recognised the need to accept his "real burden," he does not expect anyone to take responsibility for him. The novella, thus, appears to close with an implicit assurance that Wilhelm will outgrow his obsession with his victimhood and find an adequate justification for living.

CHAPTER 4

The Adventurers

A temperamental boisterousness and a refusal to give up hope differentiates Augie March and Eugene Henderson from Joseph, Leventhal, and Wilhelm. They are no less oppressed by the world or less exposed to human depravity, but it is not in their nature to be indifferent or suspicious. Touched by the problem of water contamination threatening the Arnewi village, Henderson volunteers unsolicited help, and Augie, talking to Clem, rejects the state of mind that is for ever involved in deciphering ulterior motives behind human actions. "You can always find bad motives," he says, "There are always bad motives. So all I can say is I don't want to have them" (*AM*, p. 457). Like all Bellow heroes, Augie and Henderson have a spark of idealism: Augie is keen to establish a home for orphans, and Henderson returns from Africa with a homeless boy with plans to adopt him. The adventurers are essentially innocent and try to go beyond clutter and complexity. Henderson is touched by the Biblical truth of the lilies of the field outshining Solomon, and Augie finds that his "special thing," his fixation, is simplicity. It is another matter that in desiring simplicity and denying complexity "I was guileful and suppressed many patents in my secret heart, and was as devising as anybody else" (*AM*, p. 402).

In their search for reality, Augie and Henderson elude the definitions and lifestyles offered by their Instructors and decline to follow the set roles that society imposes on them. Their openness to experience is a natural derivative of their hunger for freedom. They are carried ahead by the belief that every new adventure opens fresh gateways of meaning and hope. At the end of the long narrative of his varied experiences, Augie appears undeterred by his meagre accomplishments. "I may well be a flop in this line of endeavor," he says, "Columbus too thought he was a flop, probably, when they sent him back in chains. Which didn't prove there was no America" (*AM*, p. 536). Henderson confesses that he went to Africa because "Things got worse and worse and worse and pretty soon they were too complicated" (*HRK*, p. 3).

A close reading of the two novels suggests that Bellow is skeptical of such a view of experience and regards it as an offshoot of the cult of the ego. As in the case of the victim-heroes, Bellow retains the proneness of his protagonists to commit, and continue in, error, and exploits it to ironic advantage by using the first person point of view. Thus, Augie considers it vital to achieve an independent fate "Because what if what I am by name isn't good enough?" (*AM*, p. 485). It is hard for Augie to reconcile his conception of a "good enough" self with the demands of love because the love of others always appears to obstruct his search for a unique self. Similarly, the persistent nagging of the spirit that takes Henderson to Africa essentially implies his longing to break away from the cycle of mortality and, in effect, to escape the fate common to all men.

Still, in spite of the ironies that attend their quests, Augie and Henderson come close to an identification of the sources of stability in life. Augie feels that "Truth, love, peace, bounty, usefulness, harmony" can be realised once all exertions are relaxed and the "axial lines of life" intuited. He acknowledges that "The ambition of something special and outstanding I have always had is only a boast that distorts this knowledge" (*AM*, p. 454). He does not think that the perception of life's axial lines entails any special initiation or spiritual training: "And I believe that any man at any time can come back to these axial lines ... At any time life can come together again and man be regenerated" (*AM*, *Ibid.*). Henderson, likewise, is comforted to know that "The forgiveness of sins is perpetual and righteousness first is not required" (*HRK*, p. 3) and recalls in retrospect that "Whatever gains I ever made were always due to love and nothing else" (*HRK*, p. 339).

Augie's adventures make him intensely human. He assumes

responsibility for others and cheerfully accepts the contradictions of the world. But he is withheld from religious grace because he cannot reconcile his desire for an exceptional self with selflessness. His failure is due to his inability to bridge the gap between his insights and his way of life. He continues to seek meaning through a participation in experience even though he visualises the possibility of approaching the "axial lines of life" with a cessation of striving. Mintouchian, one of his Reality Instructors, aptly expresses his dilemma:

> "... You must take your chance on what you are. And you can't sit still. I know this double poser, that if you make a move you may lose but if you sit still you will decay. But what will you lose? You will not invent better than God or nature or turn yourself into the man who lacks no gift or development before you make the move. This is not given to us" (*AM*, p. 485).

Henderson, on the contrary, moves closer to divine redemption because God, to him, is the mysterious "Something because of whom there is not Nothing" (*HRK*, p. 253). At the end of the novel, Henderson appears to have stilled his anxiety of death, and as he goes "leaping, leaping, leaping, pounding out tingling over the pure white lining of the gray Arctic silence," when the plane lands in Newfoundland for refuelling, he intimates that his "spirit's sleep" is over and that he has awakened to a new perception of the created world (*HRK*, p. 341). But since the novel employs the first person point of view, the reader must not forget that he has only Henderson's word for the promise that lies ahead.

THE ADVENTURES OF AUGIE MARCH

In writing *The Adventures of Augie March* Bellow moved away from the tradition of the "well-made novel" and sought to create a form based on the free-wheeling picaresque novel developed by Fielding and Smollett. The Flaubertian standard that he had accepted in *The Victim* appeared constricting and repressive and made it imperative for him to yield to "emotional limits that were very confining"[1] because the scrupulous attention paid by him to structure necessarily involved the sacrifice of his freedom to experiment in a more flexible fictional mode. In *Augie March*, therefore, "I kicked over the traces, wrote catch-as-catch-can, picaresque. I took my chance. The great pleasure of the book was that it came easily. All I had to do was to be there with buckets to catch it. That's why the form is loose."[2]

But it would be incorrect to assume that *Augie March* is a picaresque novel in the purest sense of the term. The novel does have superficial and obvious resemblances with the popular notion of a picaresque novel, but in reality it has greater affinity with the *Bildungsroman*. One way of making this distinction is to perceive Bellow's attitude to the various settings in the novel. Unlike *Dangling Man*, *The Victim*, and *Seize the Day*, which are specifically set in Chicago and New York. *Augie March* does not limit its action to one particular place. Augie characterises himself as "an American, Chicago born" (p. 3) and describes his upbringing in Chicago. Very soon, he moves into wider circles of experience which take him to New York, Mexico City, Paris, and other places. The change of settings contributes significantly to the shaping of Augie's consciousness and character so much so that after his Mexican interlude it is not difficult to see that a substantial change has affected his personality. But in spite of the number of experiences in a number of places that he undergoes, his quest is essentially directed at his own self. The change he seeks is not in his environment but in himself. He is, thus, different from the hero of the picaresque novel who, in Robert Alter's words, "is what he is; sometimes splendidly, sometimes ignominiously, but always confidently . . . himself."[3] Augie has greater kinship with the *Bildungsroman* because he is unsure of the sources of stability in his life and responds to experiences with the attitude of a gambler. His adventures are, as a result, without direction

That *Augie March* has a greater affinity with the *Bildungsroman* can also be seen from the fact that Augie views his life from an altered perspective, from the point of view of a changed person. Expressing his realisation that reality is so complex that it cannot be codified within the fixities of any definition, he confesses, "I see this now. At that time, not" (p. 285). Although the novel concludes with Augie's initial steps toward self-assessment, the overall tone that informs the narrative is that of a man who has retrospectively learned from his experiences or from the reflections that the experiences have inspired. For example, his contemptuous attitude to social esteem is tinged by his insight into its veneer and artificiality:

> It takes some of us a long time to find out what the price is of being in nature, and what the facts are about your tenure. How long it takes depends on how swiftly the social sugars dissolve. But when at last they do dissolve there's a different taste in your mouth, bringing different news which registers with dark astonishment and fills your eyes. And this different news is that from vast existence in some way you rise up and at any moment you may go back (p. 362).

Like any *Bildungsroman* hero, Augie comes to realise through experience that it is not possible to come to terms with life unless the darkness beneath social niceties is perceived and experienced. Such an experience is a necessary pre-condition for the "education" of the *Bildungsroman* hero because it makes him aware of the variety and depth of life. In the frame of reference of Bellow's novels, such an understanding is an important stage in the process of self-discovery in which the protagonist is involved. Thus, the spirit of the *Bildungsroman* appears more suited to Bellow's purposes in *Augie March*.

The sprawling and aimless quality of Augie's quest determines, to a large extent, the loose form of the novel, and it is appropriate to wonder if the novel operates on an organising principle. The nature of the theme precludes the discovery of an organising principle in a sequence of causally connected events. The form of the novel can be best apprehended in terms of the relationships that govern Augie's life at given points of time. Since Augie does not wish to assume a structure of pesonality designed by someone else, he seeks the freedom to develop his own lifestyle and to understand himself without being imposed upon by his Reality Instructors. This is the central faith which sustains his ebullient quest for freedom and lends it whatever formal organisation it has.

The nature of Augie's quest is indicated at the start of the novel in the peculiar circumstances of his upbringing in a ghetto in Chicago. Raised in a Jewish matriarchal home, he comes under the influence of Grandma Lausch, his first Reality Instructor. Grandma Lausch, the reader infers, originally entered the home of the Marches as a boarder but eventually took over its management through the force of her personality. In the power she wielded over the family and the startegems she devised to use the children to extract benefits from public institutions can be seen the seeds of Augie's built-in resistance against syndromes of power reposed in individuals and his desire to enter into relationships with others in such a way that his own individuality and identity may not be compromised. In making a bid for self-sustaining independence, he refuses to allow his identity to be disguised by anything that is false, or by anything that will force him to deviate from his real purposes. He is, in effect, on the lookout for some inner order by which he may define his life, a new order which may give content to his freedom and to his adventurous spirit It is an order which all Bellow heroes look for in one way or another:

> Our period has been created by revolutions of all kinds—political, scientific, industrial. And now we have been freed by law from slavery in many of its historical, objective forms. The next move is up to us. Each of us has to find an inner law by which he can live. Without this, objective freedom only destroys us. So the question that really interests me is the question of spiritual freedom in the individual--the power to endure our own humanity.[4]

Much of the excitement and intensity of the narrative derives from the way Augie relates to particular experiences or adventures. It is thus that experience acts as a point of reference to his character and fate. Bellow frequently employs the terms, character and fate, to express the essential particulars of Augie's wanderings. When the novel begins, Augie quotes Heraclitus' aphorism, "A man's character is his fate," only to reverse it later by saying that "A man's fate is also his character." Initially Augie would have the reader believe that whatever constitutes his self or character is that which accounts for what happens to him. He would, of course, prefer his character to dominate his fate, so that his self is not submerged by the strange happenings of his life. But at the end of the novel, after his confusing and aimless wanderings, he reticently concedes that his experiences also condition his nature. Once he is in the thick of an adventure or a relationship, his behaviour-pattern is very likely to be influenced by that adventure or relationship. His conflict, therefore, concerns the search for a proper balance between character and fate. It is true that he cannot develop his character without immersion in life, but it is equally true that he cannot immerse so fully as to drown in a particular experience.

Augie's attitude to experience is one of openness. He accepts it without pre-meditation as he has no clear idea of its intrinsic worth. His problems are a function of his nature: being alive to all possibilities, he can readily be drafted by others to serve their needs: "I am constantly meeting those persons who persistently arise before me with counsels and illumination throughout my earthly pilgrimage," (p. 478) he says, but it must be borne in mind that those persons nearly always have their own needs in view. Thus, Augie finds himself on the horns of a dilemma: in order to preserve his identity, he must inevitably grant recognition to human ties; but once he has done so, his own freedom is in peril. His relationship with others must, consequently, be tenuous and uncommitted. Robert Penn Warren has perceptively noted Augie's inability to commit himself,[5] but he fails to recognise that this lack of commitment has to be judged in the light of the selfishness of others. The freedom Augie seeks is directly proportional to his refusal to grant total anthority to others on his own life.

The notion of confronting the protagonist with Reality Instructors, who try to remould his personality and conduct on the basis of their own view of reality, seems to have been borrowed by Bellow from Thomas Mann's novel *The Magic Mountain*.[6] In Mann's novel, the protagonist Hans Castorp is endlessly badgered by the eloquent but inherently conflicting value-systems of two pedagogues, Settembrini and Naphta, each of whom stakes a claim on his intellect and sensibility. Even though impressed by their rhetoric, he approaches the threshold of his own awareness of life by rising above their intricate metaphysical statements and counterstatements. Bellow's early attempt to chart out an identical pattern of self-development can be discerned in his story "Trip to Galena,"[7] published in 1950. Weyl, the hero of the story, shares the predicament of Augie. An effort is made by Weyl's sister Fanny to make him marry in the family of her fiance. But in reality, Fanny appears to be merely using him for consolidating her own security. He realises, finally, that he must act on his own, "from the heart, from attachment to life despite the worst it has shown us, and it has shown us just about everything."[8] It must, however, be pointed out that Weyl's view of life is far more pessimistic than Augie's even though they find themselves entangled in common problems. In *Augie March*, published three years after "Trip to Galena," Bellow exchanged the gloomy Weyl for the ebullient Augie, giving him the larkiness which was denied to Weyl. This shift to comedy also marks the beginning of a new phase that was to give a significant dimension to Bellow's concern with the problem of affirmation. Comedy serves to discard the solemn idea-clusters of the Reality Instructors through spoofing, creating the sense that reality is so involved and complex, so dispersed and overwhelming, that it cannot be shaped by the ideas and attitudes of any single man. The complicated reality of life is proved by the comic fact that each interpretation of its nature is mocked by its opposite.

This sense is made available to the reader in the various relationships into which Augie stumbles. The individual at the centre of each relationship is termed a "Machiavellian" because of his ability to employ his ideas and personality for the purpose of manipulating and controlling others. Externally, these "Machiavellians" appear to be composed and authoritative. Old, eccentric, crippled, or highly neurotic, they seem capable of influencing the fate of others to their advantage. Augie insightfully refers to Grandma Lausch "as one sovereign who knew exactly the proportions of love, respect, and fear of power in her subjects" (p. 6). Highly unsentimental and alive to self-interest, she saw the feeling of love as a deception which in the long run injured more than offered any good. Augie's problems appeared to demonstrate to her the troublesome fate of people who were handy with their affections: "The more you love people, the more they mix you up. A child loves, a person respects" (p. 9).

Augie has been fascinated by the Machiavellians from his

childhood. Each of them represents traits which attract as well as repel him; these people significantly enlarge his experience of the world, but he also detects blemishes in their character that he would like to do without in himself. In incident after incident the reader perceives that Augie's dormant integrity comes in the way of his total reliance on his Reality Instructors: as a budding crook he is a failure, and as a young businessman selling newspapers at a Chicago train station he finds it hard to cheat his customers as instructed. Augie's inability to accept the Machiavellian strategems leads him to confess, subsequently, that his character, his sensitive "good" nature, is his fate.

Mrs. Renling, a rich Evanston aristocrat, seeks to govern Augie by adopting him because she is keen to have a son who would be regarded as "a fashionable man about town." Augie is undoubtedly tempted by the possibility of leading a rich and comfortable life: "The situation was that I was enjoying what a rich young man enjoys," he says, "and arranged my feelings accordingly, filling in and plastering over objections" (p. 137). But what prevents Augie from accepting his new role is his independent nature : he finally realises that it would be impossible for him "to be built into Mrs. Renling's world, to consolidete what she affirmed she was" (p. 151). Mrs. Renling desires to show Augie off as a protege. She is not able to understand what Augie understands instinctively—that to possess another person completely is to deny his innate freedom. It is inevitable that Augie must step out of the magic-circle that Mrs. Renling has built around him.

Augie's brother Simon also tries to draw him into his own orbit—and not for reasons of pure brotherly affection. Although Simon, as compared to his younger brother, has achieved greater worldly success, he is intrigued by Augie's ability to live without the usual necessities of a comfortable life. He feels a need not only to guide Augie in the tricks of acquiring wealth, but also to master his life and dictate to him the rudiments of a prosperous life that most people cherish. Simon would obviously feel more secure if Augie were fashioned after his own image, as a prototype of the ordinary wealth-seeker. Augie is dissuaded from following Simon's example because of his desire to lead a free life and also because of his keen awareness of his elder brother's vulnerability to the kinds of spiritual compromises that have to be made in the pursuit of riches.

But there are other Reality Instructors also. Augie is conscious that he is "available to everybody and assuming about others what I assumed about myself" (p. 197). Einhorn, who employs Augie as a junior factotum, offers him his own lessons on the mastery of life. Mimi Villars uses him for her strange errands, and Bateshaw, a mad scientist whom Augie meets in a lifeboat, offers him the promise of life and power if he will only agree to propagate his weird scientific projects to save mankind. But Augie continues to drift away from these attempts to transform his life and conduct. "Why," he asks, "should I turn into one of these people who didn't know who they themselves were ?" (p. 151). After giving up his assignment as a union organiser, he confesses: "I couldn't just order myself to become one of those peoples who go out before the rest, who stand and intercept the big social ray, or collect and concentrate it like burning glass, who glow and dazzle and make bursts of fire. It wasn't what I was meant to be" (p. 310).

Augie's resilience extends even to the institution of marriage. He is hardly married for two days when he sets out on a new adventure across half the world. At the end of the novel, he is found conducting black market trading while his wife, Stella, pursues her career in acting elsewhere. The goals he had set for his wedded life have all disappeared : he does not even hope to build the foster home that he had dreamed about. His life continues to spin into and out of new adventures. He has not found a secure tether or a stillpoint, but he has been able to view his moral situation with a certain amount of clarity. He has also acquired an understanding of the minute movements of his own being:

> I said when I started to make the record that I would be plain and heed the knocks as they come, and also that a man's character was his fate . . . Well, then it is obvious that this fate, or what he settles for, is also his character. And since I never have had any place of rest, it should follow that I have trouble being still, and furthermore my hope is based on getting to be still so that the axial lines can be found. When striving stops, the truth comes as a gift— bounty, harmony, love, and so forth. Maybe I can't take

these very things I want (p. 514).

Augie rightly infers that his life would reach fulfilment in proximity to, what he calls, the axial lines, but the novel offers little hope or prospect of such a fulfilment or realisation. The only affirmation that the novel offers is located in Augie's intuitive grasp of the terms of spiritual fulfilment. At the end of the novel, he is still involved in experience, but he has taken stock of his situation and measured his possibilities. One is inclinded to suspect that beneath Augie's search for new kinds of experiences lurks a gnawing anxiety, an anxiety that has its roots in his failure to provide a stable and integrated focus to his own life. There is little doubt that he is frustrated by his inability to work out any satisfactory conception of self: at every turn he finds that he is being shaped not by powers residing within himself, but by social pressures, by chance, by the force of other personalities, in short, by those factors which are broadly said to constitute "fate." This anxiety relates him to the victim-heroes; his ability to observe his own situation with clarity suggests his affinity with the survivor-heroes. What Bellow seems to highlight in Augie's predicament is the problem faced by the individual in preserving his identity in a selfish society: "It takes some of us a long time to find out what the price is of being in nature, and what the facts are about your tenure" (p. 362). In refusing to surrender his larky spirit to fate, he has perforce accepted his role as an adventurer in order to achieve a balance between the demands of his free spirit and the inscrutable workings of his fate. Bellow drew attention to this fact while commenting upon the novel: "We are called upon to preserve our humanity in circumstances of rapid change and movement. I do not see what else we can do than refuse to be condemned with a time or place. We are not born to be condemned but to live."[9]

Augie's stance is, however, not without an element of error. Just as the victim-heroes regard their victimhood as a natural outcome of the dehumanising power of society, Augie believes that he must be as scheming as the Machiavellians to preserve his freedom. In one of the most revealing passages in the novel, he says:

But then with everyone going around so capable and purposeful in his strong handsome case, can you let yourself limp in feeble and poor, some silly creature, laughing and harmless ? No, you have to plot in your heart to come out differently. External life being so mighty, the instruments so huge and terrible, the performances so great, the thoughts so great and threatening, you produce a someone who can exist before it. You invent a man who can stand before the terrible appearance. This way he can't get justice, and he can't give justice, but he can live. And this is what mere humanity always does. It's made up of these inventors or artists, millions of them, each in his own way trying to recruit other people to play a supporting role and sustain him in make-believe ... That's the struggle of humanity, to recruit others to your version of what's real ... But the invented things never became real for me no matter how I urged myself to think they were... I wanted simplicity and denied complexity, and in this I was guileful and suppressed many patents in my secret heart, and was as devising as anybody else (pp. 401-402).

This point of view finely differentiates Augie from the survivor-heroes who develop their own system of values to resist the brutal forces of a social order that take an indifferent view of the individual's quest for happiness and stable values.

The Adventures of Augie March has the most extended time-span of all novels of Bellow. Augie's adventures are described from his early childhood until his mid-forties. It appears as if Bellow wanted to let his hero have all the freedom of time and space to negotiate a creative synthesis of adventure and vision. It is, however, doubtful if the experiment was wholly successful. Casting a backward glance at the novel, Bellow felt that the novel had perhaps become too undisciplined since the openness of the form led to a great deal of looseness. This may not have been an advantage, but there were other rewards : "Everytime I was depressed, I'd treat myself to a fantasy holiday with him."[10] The novelist's indulgence in fantasy allowed the novel to grow organically, following its own laws: "In *Augie* one of my real pleasures was having the ideas taken away from me, as it were, by the characters. They demanded to have their own existence."[11] In sum, Bellow's own reaction to the novel has to be described as mixed:

> I am grateful to the book because it was so liberating to write it. But I do not consider it a success. I only just discovered a new possibility. I was incapable at the time of controlling it and it ran away with me. I feel that Augie was too effusive and uncritical. But it does reflect one side of my character.[12]

The open-endedness of the novel accounts for its episodic character, its length, and the unrelatedness of several adventures to the main theme. These flaws cause a thematic and structural imbalance that several critics have noted. Leslie Fiedler called it "overly expansive" and Richard Chase felt disappointed because Augie was left "wavering and dangling at the end."[14] Such criticism *is* valid, but if one were asked to edit it, one may find it hard to decide which of the episodes have to be left out. Any such attempt at recasting the novel is likely to destroy its richness of experience and solidity of specification. If one were to ignore the import of the theme, one would still find the characterisations and settings overwhelmingly interesting in themselves. It is, therefore, best to treat the novel on its own terms and to see it as an important stage in the development of the style and manner for which Bellow was to receive the encomiums of critics later.

CHAPTER 5

The Survivors

Although the exuberance of Augie and Henderson liberates them to a great extent from the despair and hopelessness of the victim-heroes, it does betray a lack of maturity in their struggle with their problems. Herzog, Sammler, and Citrine do not share the "larkiness" of Augie and Henderson, but compensate for its absence in their serious concern with the situation of the individual in contemporary society. Herzog realises that the sensibility of the modern man is beset with a wilderness of questions, each centring round the problem of human survival:

> Well, for instance, what it means to be a man. In a city. In a century. In transition. In a mass. Transformed by science. Under organized power. Subject to tremendous controls. In a condition caused by mechanization. After the late failure of radical hopes. In a society that was no community and devalued the person. Owing to the multiplied powers of numbers which made the self negligible.... (*H*, p. 201).

Herzog's recovery is one response to these questions, a personal response made with the full awareness of the social, intellectual, moral, political, and religious issues that condition human existence in society. Herzog exhibits an innate potentiality to overcome his crisis through a process of corrective self-comprehension. In regarding survival as a part of the individual's obligation to life, he rises above the impotence of the victims and the naivety of the adventurers and learns to take a comic view of suffering. He accepts the ordinariness of reality that troubles the victims and the adventurers alike and recognises the necessity of cultivating ethical and religious values relevant to an age of extremity and crisis. In choosing to make a wilful movement from disease to convalescence (*H*, p. 4), he leaves little doubt that he is a mature member of the same lineage of which Joseph, Leventhal, Wilhelm, Augie, and Henderson are genuine but handicapped products.

In Herzog can be traced the image of the survivor, a latter-day figure celebrated in novels such as Bernard Malamud's *The Fixer*[1] and Alexander Solzhenitsyn's *One Day in the Life of Ivan Denisovich*.[2] Terence Des Pres notes that the survivor radically differs from the victim in his refusal "to accept his victimization as total" and in his invincible struggle against it:

> He will not, that is, accept the logic of the situation imposed upon him. . . . Prolonged and encompassing, the forces of negation may seem to *be* reality. But the survivor holds life and spirit within himself and knows, by the plain fact that he exists, a greater reality. He clings to his faith in the value and dignity of living things, and will not bow to destruction.[3]
>
> From his experience comes a special integrity and clarity of vision, and more, something close to what we speak of as the religious experience, that unique liberation and concentrated fulfilment of the saint—of those who, having passed in pain beyond family, possessions and self, will find themselves face to face in joy and in peace. . .[4]

According to Terence Des Pres, the morality evolved by the survivor is the result of his confrontation with an extreme situation, a situation arising not out of a clearly defined event but from "a condition of existence which persists beyond the ability of men to immediately alter it."[5] It requires the hero to "move beyond despair and self-pity to that fierce determination which the survivor above others knows. To come through. To keep a living soul in a living body."[6] The extremity faced by Herzog does not involve the kind of physical danger to which Yakob Bok (in *The Fixer*) and Ivan (in *One Day*) are exposed. But his situation poses the same threat to his moral essence that compels Yakob Bok and Ivan to cultivate their own strategies of survival and spiritual resistance. Herzog is so completely entrapped in his situation that "Not to burst, not to die—to stay alive, was all he could hope for" (*H*, p. 44). The basic premise of his "education" is the awareness that

> the first requirement of stability in a human being was that the said human being should really desire to exist. This is what Spinoza says. It is necessary for happiness (*felicitas*). He can't behave well (*bene agere*), or live well (*bene vivere*), if he himself doesn't want to live (*H*, p. 96).

Sammler, on the other hand, has been exposed to two kinds of extremity. The first—concerning the novel's present—is the state of American society that puts the normalcy of an individual under great strain. The second—referring to Sammler's past—is the situation he faced in Poland following the massacre of the Jews. Bellow dramatises Sammler's response to American society against the background of the symbolic event of the Apollo flight to the moon, and it is in the context of this response that the values cultivated by him during the war in Poland gain their special relevance and poignancy. Sammler holds life precious, but believes that it cannot be preserved significantly unless the existing notions of authenticity are inverted. Authenticity inheres, in Sammler's view, in a life of duty, virtue, and disinterestedness, in a life untroubled by finitude and ordinariness, rather than in an incessant thirst for the illimitable and an irresponsible disgust with the earth that the moon-voyage signifies.

Sammler, like Herzog, also makes an essentially personal response to the question of human survival. But the love he bears to *his* species and *his* earth give a planetary character to his thoughts. It may be said that his realisation that responses to such a vital question remain personal and isolated is the main cause of his anguished affirmation of life on a planet that sometimes appears not to respect life at all.

Humboldt's Gift, though not radically different in form, theme, and sensibility from the other two survivor-novels, does offer renewed evidence of Bellow's artistic gifts. Based on the life of Delmore Schwartz,[7] the novel touchingly dramatises an individual's attempt to bring order to his life by reconsidering the predicament of another human being. Musing upon the fate of his friend, the failed poet Humboldt, Charlie Citrine, the protagonist, comes to realise that the pre-requisites of a fulfilled life are stability, tranquillity, poise, unmotivated goodness, and creativity. Humboldt's career ended in dissipation because "he couldn't find the next thing, the new thing, the necessary thing for poets to do" (*HG*, p. 155). In desperation, he "threw himself into weakness" and, like Hoberly and Nachman in *Herzog*, became "a hero of wretchedness" (*HG, Ibid.*). Citrine's understanding of his friend's error prevents him, at crucial moments of his life, from surrendering himself to identical stances of wretchedness. When Renata, his lady-friend, deserts him for another man, he learns to accept his misfortune with calm. Taken into custody on false charges, in a dramatic situation strongly reminiscent of *Herzog*, he avoids violent exhortations and appeals to reason, conscious that he is not in a Shakespearean situation and must act with restraint and propriety.

Struggling to seek a release from the illusions of his own cluttered life, Citrine experiences the bitter disenchantment of "an arctic survivor in a small boat, an Amundsen hailing ships on the horizon which turned out to be icebergs" (*HG*, p. 158). The nature of the deceptions with which he lives is not, however, hard to identify. Like all Bellow characters in error, he is obsessed by the need to seek a special destiny, to manipulate others, and to assert his intellectual and sexual supremacy. His dreams of self-aggrandizement, in which he sees himself as an ever-victorious racquet-champion, are an unconscious manifestation of his latent paranoia (*HG*, p 109). Another related aspect of his self-love in his fear of abandonment, aging, and death. Disillusioned by Renata's betrayal, he tries to imagine her with her new lover and discovers that he "Wouldn't tolerate being wrung abandoned sea-sick shipwrecked castaway" (*HG*, p. 412). Hearing a humourous report of funeral-parlour salesmanship, he compulsively pictures himself being "put down to suffocate and rot under the weight of clay and stones—no, under sand" (*HG*, p. 197). Proficient though he is in the game of ideas, he realises that his habit of classifying all problems into neat intellectual categories doesn't "take the death-curse off for me" (*HG, Ibid.*); as a result, he continues to be haunted by the image of "a different Citrine, this one on the border of senility" being "pushed in a wheelchair past the little salt ripples, ripples which, like myself, were puny" (*HG*, p. 9).

Such fears are particularly aggravated because of his feeling that his life has not been charged with any urgent sense of purpose. Bellow employs the image of the missed boat to convey Citrine's overwhelming disgust with "the plastered idols of the Appearances" (*HG*, p. 16) and his feeling that he knows "nothing I really needed to know" (*HG*, p. 50):

> ... I had waited many thousands of years for God to send my soul to this earth ? Here I was supposed to capture a true and clear word before I returned, as my human day ended. I was afraid to go back empty-handed. Being sensible could do absolutely nothing to mitigate this fear of missing the boat (*HG*, p. 199).

Citrine turns to Rudolf Steiner's ideas on anthroposophy to establish contact with a higher order of reality. Although his attachment to this school of speculation about cosmic memory and spiritual transcendence is touching to the point of tedium, the reader cannot escape the feeling that Bellow's own reaction to Steiner is at once deliberately serious and playful. To take an example, if Citrine is made to say at one time that his new discipline has begun to manifest its "good effects" (*HG*, p. 189), he is also made to reverse the credibility of the statement at another time through an involuntary confession that the learned theosophist's esoteric texts made him "uneasy" and "set my teeth on edge. I said to myself, this is lunacy" (*HG*, p. 439). Bellow's ambivalence enables him to provide a vivid account of his protagonist's hunger for a new and more purposive beginning; at the same time, through a network of covert ironies underlying the plot, he seems to hint that the solutions believed valid by Citrine are not entirely untainted and, at times, cut him off from reality. As Citrine's mind soars away from the drudgery of ordinary existence, he is often found napping on important personal matters (*HG*, p. 439). Bellow, thus, succeeds in maintaining a paradoxical attitude toward Citrine's conflict by constantly overturning his ideas and, thereby, strengthening their essential comic function.

The contrariness of ideas and stances, implicit as it is in the structure of the novel, does not, however, suppress certain dominant thematic resonances. The most important of these relates to Citrine's agonised search for meaning and significance in a life rendered sterile by unreality and self-deception. Bellow appears to suggest that it is possible to imbue human life with significance through an acceptance of the complex ordinariness of reality, without subjecting it to the reductive processes of intellection. The quest for an interesting or exceptional life is, therefore, vain and futile. Citrine's "education" stems from the recognition that he does not have to make himself interesting "through madness, eccentricity, or anything of the sort" because "the power to cancel the world's distortions, activity, noise, and become fit to hear the essence of things" resides within each individual and is as natural to the soul as the root is to the flower (*HG*, p. 312). The nature of reality can be intuited and deciphered if the individual allows the "deepest elements" within the self to "disclose their deepest information" (*HG*, p. 357). Then,

> If there is nothing but non-being and oblivion waiting for us, the prevailing beliefs have not misled us, and that's that.... Suppose, however, that oblivion is not thec ase (*HG, Ibid.*) ?

The rhetorical question about death's ultimacy in the passage quoted above tends to direct Bellow's concern with the problem of human survival to an area of spiritual inquiry dealing with after-life and the immortality of the human soul. Obsessed by the ineluctability of transience, Citrine, like Herzog and Sammler (*H*, p. 314; *SP*, p. 236), constantly speculates on the fate of the soul after death. Is death the denial or cessation of human possibilities, he wonders ? Or, are there some fields of consciousness, as yet unexplored, that continue to transmit meaning after death (*HG*, p. 263) ? Although his cerebration in these matters remains inconclusive, he reaches over to a state of tranquillity by realising, through the example of the success and popularity of a scenario on which Humboldt had collaborated with him, that the power of real talent and creativity can be felt even beyond the barrier of life and the trappings of worldly success. Humboldt's gift to Citrine, therefore, involves a new perception, a fresh lease of life : it affirms that the soul survives through the potency of the imagination to retrieve the hidden truths abiding in the universe : "The imagination must not pine away—that was Humboldt's message. It must assert again that art manifests the inner powers of nature" (p. 112). Bellow communicates Citrine's recognition of this truth symbolically through the image of the tiny crocus flowering in the New Jersey cemetery where a decent re-burial for Humboldt has been arranged. It is true that Citrine's personality has not undergone a complete transformation and that his material problems remain what they are, but he has taken the first firm step in a direction lighted with spiritual possibilities. There is, therefore, the hope that he would weather his crisis and replenish his spiritual energy.

HERZOG

The broadest fictional category in which *Herzog* may be placed is that of the Menippean Satire. According to Northrop Frye, the Menippean satirist is concerned more with intellectual themes and attitudes than with dramatic action. He deals with "Pedants, bigots, cranks, parvenus, virtuosi, enthusiasts, rapacious and incompetent professional men of all kinds"[1] and shows "his exuberance in intellectual ways, by piling up an enormous mass of erudition about his theme or in overwhelming his pedantic targets with an avalanche of their own jargon."[2] His chief target of ridicule is the *philosophus gloriosus* because evil and folly are to him "diseases of the intellect," "a kind of maddened pedantry which the *philosophus gloriosus* at once symbolizes and defines."[3]

The satire in *Herzog* is mainly directed against its chief protagonist, Moses Elkanah Herzog, a middle-aged professor of political philosophy, whose ambition was to provide "a new angle on the modern condition, showing how life could be lived by renewing universal connections ; overturning the law of the Romantic errors about the uniqueness of the self; revising the old Western, Faustian ideology, investigating the social meaning of Nothingness. And more" (p. 39). His second divorce throws him off-balance, his research is abandoned, and, in a state of mental instability, he writes, but rarely mails, letters to persons dead and alive, and scribbles notes for himself on instant impulse to contain his inner disquiet. The act of writing letters is constantly invaded by a flood of reminiscences, mostly about people to whom the letters are written, to light up specific incidents from the past. A *philosophus gloriosus* in his own right, who believed that "the progress of civilization—indeed the survival of civilization—depended on . . . (his) successes" (p. 125), Herzog gradually learns to spoof and outgrow his ego-centricity and achieves comprehension of a system of values that may lend meaning to existence—his own and that of others.

The design employed by Bellow to trace the course of Herzog's recovery depends on a quick transition from the present to the past. The present describes Herzog on the point of self-knowledge in his country-house in Ludeyville reviewing his past which extends over several layers of memory, and offers a quick glimpse of his childhood, adulthood, intellectual achievements, romantic escapades, marriages, divorces, and crisis. The main action of the novel is mapped out over five days immediately preceding Herzog's return to Ludeyville. It recounts his trip to Vineyard Haven for a vacation on medical advice and his quick return to New York (*Chapters II-III*); his moment of intimacy with Ramona, his lady-friend (*Chapter V*); his visit to the court to meet his lawyer, his presence during four criminal trials, and his decision to go to Chicago to murder his ex-wife's paramour (*Chapter VI*); his change of heart after watching the lover give a bath to his daughter (*Chapter VII*); his involvement in a car accident and release from police-custody (*Chapter VIII*); and his return to Ludeyville (*Chapter IX*). Herzog's train-journey to Vineyard Haven (*Chapters II-III*), his arrival in New York and his visit to Ramona (*Chapters VI-V*), and his stay in Ludeyville till his brother's arrival (*Chapter IX*) provide exclusive occasions for his letters. Cerebration, thus, occupies the greater length of the novel and forms, using Herzog's own term, a kind of "gyroscope" (p. 285). Bellow achieves a complex and delicate blend of action, memory, and thought by a careful use of three basic structural strategies—the *I-He* shifts in the narrative, the letters, and the notes. Since these devices also indicate Herzog's return to normalcy through subtle changes in attitudes and tone, a brief study of their respective functions helps to unveil Bellow's controlling intention and his method of executing it in the novel.

The *I-He* shifts in *Herzog* are a refinement of the journal-form of *Dangling Man* and an extension of the narrator-reflector relationship in *Seize the Day*. The third person point of view turns the protagonist into a subject of his own investigation, an impersonal locus of his consciousness, toward whom a variety of attitudes can be assumed. In its uncomplicated and obvious form, *he* is used for simple reporting ("He heard the crows in the morning," p. 2), self-analysis ("was he even spectacularly sick . . .?" p. 4), and self-mockery ("And without the ability to attract women, how was he to recover?" p. 5). Sometimes, however, *he* is transformed into the impersonal referent *you* ("Very well, Moshe Herzog—if you must be pitiable, sue for aid and succor . . . ," p. 86) and, in a mood of extreme dejection, even *that* ("That suffering joker," p. 11). As a *pro-form*, *he* serves for Herzog's short, professional, and family names; the proper names, when prefixed or suffixed to words such as "professor," "amorous," "squire," and "marvelous" point to the different roles assumed by him to confront reality. On such occasions, the context usually determines the tone of irony, self-ridicule, or self-pity that Herzog reserves for himself.

The shift from *he* to *I* in the narrative helps to achieve the intensity of self-articulation characteristic of the first person point of view. The shift also dramatises Herzog's participation in some event whose scope and value is to be kept restricted from him. The author is, thus, distanced from any stances that the protagonist may self-righteously assume.

Herzog's letters are a part of his "curious project of attempted communication" (p. 162). They show him acting out the roles of son, brother, lover, ex-husband, son-in-law, relative, friend, patient, host, writer, professor, intellectual, observer, property-owner, client, childhood friend, playmate, and cadet. Separated from the main narrative typographically and by an idiom growing out of Herzog's intellectual orientation, the letters are frequently interrupted by memories of persons, events, and situations. Since an awareness of the addressee very often determines the manner of the letter, Herzog's tone is querulous, bitter, sad, playful, desperate, businesslike, and erratic, depending upon who he is writing to. His personal letters are in the nature of belated retorts to persons against whom he entertains a suspicion and grudge (Letters to Dr. Edvig, Lawyer Sandor Himmelstein, and Aunt Zelda). At times the pressure of feeling gets the better of Herzog and makes even a routine business-letter digress into a discussion of personal problems. For example, the letter to Marshall Field & Co., meant to disown responsibility for credit extended to his divorced wife, goes on to say "*Of course I should have written sooner . . . but I temporarily lost my bearings*" (p. 47).

The power that dominates Herzog's letters is singularly lacking in his image as an individual. This is due to the comic dichotomy in his personality resulting from his adoption of different roles—that of a sufferer and that of an aggressive *philosophus gloriosus* - in personal and intellectual spheres. Herzog's recovery at the end of the novel is marked by a lessening of the gap between the roles assumed by him. As a result, he also becomes aware of the futility of theorising and begins to show a greater humility in his letters.

Like the letters, Herzog's notes are an index of his attempts to find poise and balance. Involuntary, urgent, cryptic, and funny, they are often a comment on himself, a telegraphic judgment containing "necessary words only." They frequently employ a conceit to voice Herzog's self-criticism: "*On the knees of your soul ? Might as well be useful. Scrub the floor*" (p. 3). Sometimes, by imitating journalistic usage they also tend to become "objective correlatives" of his need to survive: "*It has been reported . . . that several teams of Russian Cosmonauts have been lost; disintegrated, we must assume. One was heard calling 'SOS—world SOS.' Soviet confirmation has been withheld*" (p. 11). The notes are not discursive or argumentative like most of the letters; they are subjective to the point of being idiosyncratic and express the immediacy with which an idea seizes Herzog. They are also useful in suggesting the different phases of his recovery. Following his self-realisation, they take the form of prayer: "*Lord, I ran to fight in Thy holy cause, but kept tripping, never reached the scene of the struggle*" (p. 128). At the end of the novel, the notes become resolutions and are free from the eccentricities that Herzog used earlier as a front against chaos;

"*I will do no more to enact the peculiarities of life. This is done well enough without my special assistance*" (p. 340).

The *I-He* shifts, letters, and notes are employed by Bellow to convey a vivid sense of his protagonist's crisis. The devices make it apparent that the crisis is due to Herzog's illusions about himself and reality. Herzog's problems are real and cause him intense anguish, but his immature way of dealing with them is also the source of comedy in the novel. The letters and the notes make it plain that the comic nature of his illusion has to be understood in terms of two interrelated factors concerning his personal as well as professional life. He views his broken marriage as a challenge, a defeat that he seeks to turn into victory by taking up the posture of an innocent, aggrieved, and suffering person against his ex-wife Madeleine and her paramour Valentine Gersbach (p. 10). The gap between Herzog's assumed role and his real feelings is suggested by the images of mental violence which seize him when Madeleine announces her decision to divorce him, and by his hypochondria which he uses to solicit the sympathy of others. Retaining a calm exterior, Herzog pictures "what might have happened if instead of listening so intensely and thoughtfully he had hit Madeleine in the face . . . What if he had!" (pp. 9-10). Hoping "for some definite sickness" to help him absorb the impact of his crisis, he visits Dr. Emmerich, who finds nothing seriously wrong with him. The strength of his constitution belies his role as a sick man and he realises, in retrospect, that he had gone "to Emmerich to accuss Madeleine, or simply to talk about her with someone who knew her and could take a realistic view of her" (p. 14).

Herzog's bitterness is aggravated by his paranoiac belief that he is a pioneer-thinker on a mission to correct certain basic fallacies in the history of ideas and that in mistreating him, "Madeleine injured a great project" (p. 123). His letter to Monsignor Hilton makes a succinct statement of his academic ambitions:

> *And the peculiar idea entered my (jewish) mind that we'd see about this : My life would prove a different point altogether. Very tired of the modern form of historicism which sees in this civilization . . . what Heidegger calls the second fall of Man into the quotidian or ordinary. No philosopher knows*

what the ordinary is, has not fallen into it deeply enough. The question of ordinary human experience is the principal question of these modern centuries, as Montaigne and Pascal, otherwise in disagreement, both clearly saw.—The strength of a man's virtue or spiritual capacity measured by his ordinary life.

One way or another the no doubt mad idea entered my mind that my own actions had historic importance, and this (fantasy?) made it appear that people who harmed me were interfering with an important experiment (p. 106).

Subjecting others as well as himself to his unsparing scrutiny and analysis, Herzog blames the instinct of categorising, intellectualising, and explaining phenomena for clouding man's perception of reality. "But can thought wake you from the dream of existence?" he asks, "Not if it becomes a second realm of confusion, another more complicated dream, the dream of intellect, the delusion of total *explanations*"(p. 166). Lessons in reality thus conceived acquire the character of fixations, intended to shape personality on set notions of what life is like. Herzog is repelled by the insistence on imparting such a wisdom because he considers it another form of madness : *"A very special sort of lunatic expects to inculcate his principles. . . . Reality Instructors. They want to teach you—to punish you with—the lessons of the Real"* (p. 125).

The Reality Instructors against whom Herzog reserves his strongest suspicions are of two types : those who wish to influence his private life (Simkin, Sandor Himmelstein, Edvig, Valentine Gersbach, and Ramona) and those who hope to interpret and alter human history with their own special slant or inclination (Shapiro, Mermelstein, Heidegger, and others). Each of the Reality Instructors proposes a lifestyle or a philosophy of conduct whose persuasive charm Herzog tries to defy in order to locate his own bearings. The lessons offered to him are deceptive, seeking either to compromise his freedom or to cheat him outright. Simkin and Sandor Himmelstein, the two lawyers, and Edvig, the psychiatrist, whom he consults after his divorce, stand for different attitudes to realism. Simkin is a "practical realist" : while asking Herzog to enter into litigation with his ex-wife, he indirectly incites him to take revenge on her lover. Sandor Himmelstein, who enjoys torturing other people in the name of being realistic, believes that the truth of facts depends upon their intrinsic nastiness (p. 86). Under the pretence of sympathy, he turns over the money Herzog had left with him for an emergency to Madeleine. Herzog suspects that Edvig, while treating him, fell in love with Madeleine and aided her in getting rid of him. His greatest grudge is against Valentine Gersbach, his former friend, who seduced Madeleine and tried to console him with Martin Buber's philosophy of "I and Thou." Herzog notes with biting irony how Buber's thought can be perverted into a tactics of adultery:

I'm sure you know the views of Buber. It is wrong to turn a man (a subject) into a thing (an object). By means of a spiritual dialogue, the I-It relationship becomes an I-Thou relationship. God comes and goes in man's soul. And men come and go in each other's souls. Sometimes they come and go in each other's beds, too. You have dialogue with a man. You have intercourse with his wife (p. 64).

As compared to Simkin, Sandor, Edvig, and Gersbach, Ramona Donsell, Herzog's lady-friend after his divorce, is genuinely concerned with his plight and is keen to "restore order and clarity to his life" (p. 185). Herzog entertains a mild suspicion that her willingness to come to his aid may be due to her desire to marry him; but, more important, he finds it hard to share her belief that a satisfying sexual relationship would cure him of all his problems. Although her company brings him temporary peace, he never really brings himself to agree with her way of life. He is on a different search, and sex, he knows, does not answer his "higher problems" : "is that the secret goal of my vague pilgrimage ?" he asks himself, "Do I see myself to be after long blundering an unrecognized son of Sodom and Dionysus—an Orphic type ?" (p. 17).

Herzog's distrust of theorising determines his response to the Reality Instructors of the academic world. The method he employs to demolish their stances is Socratic in spirit. As a first step he exposes an intellectual formulation by creating an honest doubt about its validity through innocent, but ironic, questioning; then, as a second step, he carefully introduces his own standpoint after eliminating all other alternatives as logically or ethically untenable. The arguments contested by Herzog invariably centre round the state of the present-day civilisation and the place of man in it: his aim is almost always to reject theories that decry modern society and to affirm man's possibilities of transcendence by hinting at a system of values that, in his view, characterises—or ought to characterise—human life.

Containing a curious admixture of insight and error, the passage quoted above stresses an important source of Herzog's illusion. Earnestly seeking the knowledge of reality, he recognises that a comparison between the exaggerated ordinariness of the present and the imagined glory of the past has led historians to underrate contemporary society. Inverting the emphasis of such cliche notions, Herzog asserts, paraphrasing Kierkegaard,[4] that the ordinary is the measure of a man's virtue and vitality. The irony is that in upholding ordinariness Herzog begins to regard himself as an extraordinary person on whose intellectual prowess depends the continuance of civilisation : "But of course he, Herzog, predictably bucking such trends, had characteristically, obstinately, defiantly, blindly but without sufficient courage or intelligence tried to be a *marvelous* Herzog, a Herzog who, perhaps clumsily, tried to live out marvellous qualities vaguely comprehended" (p. 93).

Herzog's desire for uniqueness, when allowed expression, gives him the airs of a *genius domas*, and, when frustrated, creates a vacuum which the role of the sufferer only partially helps to fill. The novel dramatises the point in his life when, tired of inauthenticity and conscious that "he had mismanaged everything" (p. 3), he is "overcome by the need to explain, to have it out, to justify, to put in perspective, to clarify, to make amends" (p. 2). His quest for authenticity is in response to his much dreaded "depths of feeling" which can no longer be assuaged by the roles he has constructed for himself (p. 10). Although he realises that his life was, "as the phrase goes, ruined" (p. 3), he has no wish to choose death as an alternative : "His duty was to live. To be sane, and to live, and to look after the kids" (p. 27). Condemned, thus, to survive, his great need is to confront reality, to probe the sources of stability in life, and to try to know what it means to be human. In this endeavour, *it may seem* that his ideas and actions serve a complementary function because the peculiar circumstances of his life have endowed him with a double insight : as an intellectual, he is conscious of the widespread distrust and subversion of human possibilities in our time; and, as an individual, he feels engulfed by a moral chaos threatening these very qualities within him. In reality, however, his ideas, by insisting on marvellous conduct, have tended to take him away from reality toward greater ego-centricity and inauthenticity. Bellow's comic view of Herzog is integral to this incongruity of ideas and actions, to the individul's dependence on the theoretician for survival. It becomes inevitable for Herzog to realise that his hunger for marvellous qualities, his attempt to mould his life on abstract ideas, has imprisoned him in a "shameless and impotent privacy."[5] His recovery accompanies the awareness that human existence does not become meaningful by role-acting, by more attempts to live out ideas, and that reality outsteps all its intellectual versions. In this sense, the novel moves beyond definitions and theories, beyond the reach of thought and explanations as it were, to affirm life freed from all intellectual categories.

Herzog's struggle to overcome his crisis and comprehend the meaning of reality is phased by Bellow in terms of four *revelatory processes*. These may be broadly captioned as (i) discernment through analysis, (ii) memory, (iii) moral analogues, and (iv) action. There is no sequential priority in the choice of these processes in the narrative; there is also no neat separation of one process from the other so that they even intersect and overlap to evoke a sense of urgency and conflict; and, finally, each of these has a specific function to perform in bringing Herzog to the first step of the self-knowledge with which any *Bildungsroman*—to employ Bellow's term for the novel[6]—often concludes.

Herzog perceives that a serious limitation of intellectual attempts to explain history results from the romanticising of events of doubtful historicity to such an excess that statements intended to be at best metaphorical begin to assume the texture of established facts. In a pungent and cryptic letter to Heidegger, he mocks the great philosopher's view of the origin of modern man's crisis as a fall *from* heroism or uniqueness *into* the quotidian or the ordinary. Putting on an innocent and bland face, Herzog asks, *"When did this fall occur ? Where were we standing when it happened ?"* (p. 49). His letter to Egbert Shapiro, likewise, questions the validity of the feeling prevalent among intellectuals and laymen that contemporary society represents the "decay of the religious foundations of civilization" (p. 74):

> *Are all the traditions used up, the beliefs done for, the consciousness of the masses not yet ready for the next development ? Is this the full crisis of dissolution ? Has the filthy moment come when moral feeling dies, conscience disintegrates, and respect for liberty, law, public decency, all the rest, collapses in cowardice, decadence, blood ? Old Proudhon's visions of darkness and evil can't be passed over. But we mustn't forget how quickly the visions of genius become the canned sauerkraut of Spengler's "Prussian Socialism," the common-places of the Wasteland outlook, the cheap mental stimulants of Alienation, the cant and rant of pipsqueaks about Inauthenticity and Forlornness. I can't accept this foolish dreariness* (pp. 74-75).

Herzog regards historical generalisations of the sort made by Heidegger and Shapiro as inherently defective because their subject is the "whole life of mankind," a *"subject ... too great, too deep for such a weakness, cowardice—too deep, too great"* (p. 75). The "aesthetic critique of history" they produce relies for its ingenious interpretations on the "standardized pedantry of the Spenglers" and on the "cunning of reason" in which the heirs of Marx and Hegel are trained (p.75). Their perspective thus distorted, the historians of ideas are cut off from reality and develop nostalgic attachment for an ideal situation of their invention, *"which they believe is the only true and the only human reality"* (p. 306). The domestication of such cultural and intellectual ideas in modern society leads to a pernicious conditioning of "civilized individuals." Sharing the populistic feeling that he inhabits a doomed civilisation, the individual is *"provoked to take revenge upon himself, a revenge of derision, contempt, denial of transcendence"* (p. 164). The self-hatred so generated suppresses human qualities, surrounding the individual on all sides with a gloom of his own making. Herzog believes that the need is to reconsider, recover, and even discover human qualities and to liberate the individual from a naive faith in the virtue of suffering. He tells Professor Mermelstein:

> *We must get it out of our heads that this is a doomed time, that we are waiting for the end, and the rest of it, mere junk from fashionable magazines. Things are grim enough without these shivery games. People frightening one another—a poor sort of moral exercise. But to get to the main point, the advocacy and the praise of suffering take us in the wrong direction and those of us who remain loyal to civilization must not go for it.* (pp. 316-317).

The conviction emerging out of Herzog's historical analysis is that reality eludes codification and that metaphysical and dialectical attempts to verbalise its nature and meaning are debased by the very conclusions with which the consciousness of man is intended to be sublimated. That Herzog considers reality *transverbal*, rooted in the depths of feeling that relate to significant human experience, is confirmed by two contrasts that he establishes in his memory. Comparing Egbert Shapiro, the academic, and his father, an apple-vendor, he rejects Shapiro's picture of modern society as unreal, but concludes that "There was more of the truth of life in those spotted, spoiled apples, and in old Shapiro, who smelled of the horse and produce, than in all of these learned references" (p. 70). He awakens to his own blindness to reality by analysing an important event of his boyhood. Absorbed in the metaphors of books such as *The World as Will and Idea* and *The Decline of the West*, Herzog took little notice of his mother's approaching death, of the supreme reality making its presence felt in his home. It was a text Herzog "chose not to read," although his mother knew that he would have to learn its lessons someday: "She only pitied me, her orphan, understood I was a gesture-maker, ambitious, a fool; thought I would need my eyesight and my strength on a certain day of reckoning" (p. 234).

Herzog is helped to an understanding of his own situation

by three moral analogues which highlight the fate of individuals virtually ruined by their obsessive fixations or choices. He re-enacts in memory the experience of Nachman, his childhood friend, who, by rejecting his environment for poetry, rejected, in effect, his own life. Nachman's choices—his love for Blake, his poverty, and his attachment to a mentally unhinged girl who eventually committed suicide—symbolise a commitment to an idealised life which has few consolations to offer because it is totally divorced from reality. Herzog's friend Luke Asphalter's love for a dead monkey provides another touching, and yet comical, analogy. Asphalter is so grief-stricken by his monkey's death that he tries to revive him by mouth-to-mouth respiration, exposing himself, in the process, to the tubercular infection of the animal. Herzog also thinks of Geroge Hoberly, Ramona's former boy-friend, who morbidly continues to wallow in failure and suffering to demonstrate his love. Herzog perceptively recognises the moral embedded in the lives of Nachman, Asphalter, and Hoberly. The desire to transform one's life on the pattern of a fixed ideal precipitates alienation, discontent, and suffering. His own life offers a striking example of this truth: his research project—his academic obsession—is in shambles and his marital situation—another of his obsessions—had led to a "humiliating comedy of heartache" (p. 166). The morning after his intimacy with Ramona, while leaving her at her shop, he suddenly discerns that love has brought him greater happiness and contentment than intellection. But once Ramona has left, he finds that aloneness has made him "again the inescapable Moses Elkanah Herzog" (p. 206). Confronted thus with a fundamental truth of authentic existence, Herzog is led to confess that "Oneself is simply grotesque" and that *"Subjective monstrosity must be overcome, must be corrected by community, by useful duty"* (p. 219).

These conclusions, however pious, are at best only tentative and lack the authority of significant personal experience. Bellow devises a series of morally determinate actions—the courtroom scenes, Herzog's subsequent attempt to murder Gersbach, and his involvement in a car accident—to bring his protagonist's recognition of reality into proper focus and to prepare the ground for his recovery. The actions are triggered by Herzog's reaction to a letter written by Geraldine Portnoy,

Luke Asphalter's friend, recounting how Madeleine and Gersbach once left his little daughter locked in the car while they quarrelled inside the apartment. Advised by Simkin to seek legal possession of his daughter, Herzog, killing time before his appointment with the lawyer, drifts into the court and witnesses four criminal trials involving charges of mugging, homosexual soliciting, attempted robbery, and child murder respectively. Obviously, Bellow uses Herzog's presence in the courtroom to expose him to the depravity of the human heart and, thereby, to improve and enlarge his notion of reality. But, more important, the trial interacts with Herzog's consciousness to evoke in him the same drives for evil, revenge, and murder that dominate the criminals. This parallelism is employed to modify and to give a finer balance to Herzog's theoretical assumptions about human life and to convey powerfully what it means to be human. Consequently, Herzog's cerebration in the courtroom is suspended momentarily after the third trial to introduce a moving episode from his childhood His mother, in answer to his innocent question about the creation of Adam, "rubbed the palm of her hand with a finger, rubbed until something dark appeared on the deep-lived skin, a particle of what certainly looked to him like earth" (p. 232). The mother's playful act connotes the Biblical utterance, "For dust thou art, and unto dust shall thou return," and reinforces the suggestion that the fact of man really being dust lends all his material strivings the appearance of vanity. Herzog's memory of the episode is closely related to his decision to go to Chicago and take revenge on Gersbach *after* witnessing the trial of a young couple accused of child-murder. He sees in the couple a reflection of Madeleine and Gersbach, and the thought of the dead child awakens the memory of his own daughter locked in the car. The necessity of revenge is, therefore, felt instantaneously: it "was not reached; it simply arrived" (p. 241).

In contrasting the incident of Herzog's childhood with his desire to avenge himself, Bellow's aim is to dramatise the comic separation of Herzog's rational processes from his impulses. Herzog accurately identifies vanity as the root cause of man's material strivings, yet allows himself to be driven by passion when his own domestic situation is brought into question. The contrast also implies that the revenge contemplated by him is an act of pride, a plunge into greater inauthenticity and moral confusion.

But Herzog has an innate humanity that keeps his destructive instincts in check and neutralises them by forcing the realisation that his actions have been largely motivated by his ego. Face to face with the evidence that contradicts his prejudices—the sight of Gersbach giving a bath to his daughter—Herzog, in a dramatic moment of truth, grasps the vanity and absurdity of his murder-attempt. Bellow suggests through this episode that the reality sought so desperately by Herzog inheres not in his inflamed feelings or theoretical formulations, but in his acknowledgement of the possibility of love in a person whom he had bitterly and vehemently held guilty of betrayal:

> To shoot him!—an absurd thought. As soon as Herzog saw the actual person giving an actual bath, the reality of it, the tenderness of such a buffoon to a little child, his intended violence turned into *theater*, into something ludicrous. He was not ready to make such a complete fool of himself. Only self hatred could lead him to ruin himself because his heart was "broken." How could it be broken by such a pair? (p. 258).

Misjudging the mode of affirmation in *Herzog*, John W. Aldridge has complained against Bellow's "facile trick" of treating "his secondary characters as if they were inmates of either a zoo or a madhouse."[7] According to Aldridge, the difference between the protagonist and the secondary characters is obvious and simplistic—Herzog, a "quiet, deferential" man being endlessly badgered by "freaks and egomaniacs" such as Gersbach, Simkin, Shapiro, Himmelstein and others—and is meant "to provide a milieu of grotesque idiosyncrasy and self-preoccupation against which Herzog can be seen as saintly."[8] Aldridge fails to note that feelings of betrayal have so obsessed Herzog's mind that, for a while, his sense of propriety, of right and wrong has been completely blurred. In a disturbed mental state, with the moral balance tilted, there is a natural tendency on the part of the ego to reign supreme and view others as objects, as inferiors and caricatures. Immediately after his second divorce, Herzog is possessed by the infantile belief that his acquaintances either have to be on his side or on Madeleine's. Thus, he regards Gersbach, Edvig, Himmelstein, and Shapiro as charlatans. Similarly, most women seem to him to be cruel and enigmatic (pp. 41-42). But when his moral sense is restored, he is able to perceive that his conduct has been comical and that in trying to be a *philosophus gloriosus* he merely became a clown. Such a self-knowledge is an important concern of the Menippean Satire, the form to which *Herzog* belongs.

Herzog's conversation with Luke Asphalter the very evening he decides not to kill Gersbach acts as a crucial indicator of his growing self-awareness. Asphalter informs him that after his monkey's death he had tried to cure his depression and grief by practising Tina Zokoly's exercises on facing the terror of death; his meditation, however, induced only absurd visions of buttocks and burlesque girls. Herzog, struck by the comic parallel between Asphalter's and his own imbalanced actions, consoles him by pointing out that he has merely been the victim of a painful emotional comedy. Rejecting the "tension of guilt and dread as a corrective," he considers Asphalter's—and his own—absurd antics an outcome of an unemployed consciousness which abuses and ridicules itself in the absence of a clear understanding of "what to live for, what to die for" (pp. 272-273). Purposive engagement, to Herzog, does not consist in metaphysical theories that alienate man from his environment by preaching the gospel of angst. It can be discovered, on the other hand, in togetherness, in "our employment by other human beings and their employment by us" (p. 272). Metaphysical freedom cannot be achieved by turning away from others because man becomes human through brotherhood: "Man liveth not by self alone but in his brother's face .... Each shall behold the Eternal Father and love and joy abound" (p. 272).

Herzog's car-accident the next day while driving his daughter to the museum and his subsequent involvement with the police continue his exposure to reality and confirm the course of his recovery. Accused of possessing a pistol without licence, Herzog finds himself "Down in the ranks with other people—ordinary life" (p. 287) and displays a strength, dignity, and calm completely at variance with his earlier neurotic instability —"no defiance, no special pleading, nothing of the slightest personal color" (p. 294). His poise renders Madeleine's malice obvious before the sergeant who also begins to "make out her haughty peculiarities at last" (p. 301). Through such changes in Herzog's attitude, Bellow hints at strong possibilities of recovery. For once, Herzog appears resigned to the relationship between Madeleine and Gersbach. He withholds any final moral judgment on them, but accepts responsibility for the evil he had sought to inflict on their lives (p. 299). At the same time, he resolves to prevent his life from turning into "tamer forms of entertainment," a circus, or a "gladatorial combat" (p. 303). He has also developed a conception of the "dream of man's heart"; it is, he notes in a memorandum to himself before being released from police-custody, *"that life may complete itself in significant pattern. Some incomprehensible way. Before death. Not irrationally but incomprehensibly fulfilled"* (p. 303).

The reiteration of the word "incomprehensible" in Herzog's view of the "dream of man's heart" suggests an important stage in his mental development. It also helps to answer Earl Rovit's charge that "neither he nor we are able to know whether it is affirmation or sheer exhaustion that puts an end to his cerebration."[9] The word "incomprehensible" plainly refers to Herzog's ease with ambiguties and his gradual triumph over neurosis since "*neurosis might be graded by the inability to tolerate ambiguous situations*" (p. 304). But in a subtle connotation, and as distinguished from the word "irrational," it refers to a vital religious strain latent in his personality which he cultivates further on his return to his country-home. Earlier in the novel, while returning from a visit to Himmelstein, he felt moved by the power of the sun, the ocean, and the purity of air and considered if "he might beg God to make ... use of him" (p. 91). He discarded the possibility as "too simple" and "too childish" since the "actual sphere" or reality appeared to him, in comparison, different and complex, "turbulent, angry" (p. 91). Having learnt in the course of his trial that reality cannot be conceptualised and that the childishness he had criticised in religious acceptance actually lies in him, he is ineluctably drawn to make room for mysteries without keys and to affirm the system of values through which they may be approached.

Apart from the virtue of togetherness, the important elements in the system of values affirmed by Herzog are joy, humility, compassion, and acceptance. In Ludeyville, he discovers that he is "consciously cheerful" in spite of his "present loneliness" and that his independence from Madeleine involves not a sense of loss but of joy. He even writes short letters to Madeleine and Gersbach to put a stamp of good humour on his estrangement from them (pp. 313-318). He no longer needs to suffer to dramatise his predicament before others and rejects Nietzsche's ecstatic celebration of the Dionysian spirit's indulgence in evil and pain (p. 319). In a letter to Mermelstein, he claims that he is willing *"Without further exercise in pain to open my heart"* (p. 317) His refusal to enter a hospital on his brother's advice is, in his eyes, an evidence of his sanity (p. 341) and reflects the increasing clarity with which he is able to view his situation. The joy he finds in the created world makes him "share with the rats too" (p. 2), and he has the kindness of not even trying "to drive the owls out of the house" (p. 320). He is alive to his aims, but wishes to fulfil them without any further self-projection: *"I have certain things still to do And without noise, I hope"* (p. 326). He concedes his religious conversion with humility: *"The light of truth is never far away, and no human being is too negligible or corrupt to come into it* (p. 314). Placid before the inexplicable mysteries of life and death, he finds peace not in ratiocination but in prayer: *"This is the only way I have to reach out—out where it is incomprehensible"* (p. 326). He is content "to play the instrument I've got" (p. 330), and does not aspire to achieve a state of being inconsistent with what he is (p. 340). Requiring no further explanations to justify his existence, he is secure in the peace he has found— "confident cheerful, clairvoyant, and strong" (p. 1).

A comparative reading of *Herzog* and Heinrich Boll's *The Clown*[10] helps in an assessment of Bellow's achievement. Schnier, the clown of Boll's novel, has obvious affinities with Herzog. Both the protagonists have pronounced paranoiac tendencies which are exploited to comic advantage in the two novels. Schnier has been estranged from his wife because of her strong attachment to the Catholic faith. She has, like Madeleine, gone to live with her paramour Zupfner who, like Gersbach, is a charlatan, "a kind of Alcibiades of German Catholicism."[11]

Schnier, like Herzog, reacts violently to his abandonment and feels that his "business" with Zupfner can only be settled by a duel. His Ramona is Monika Silvs: his relationship with her, he confesses, is at a stage "where it would be both physically and metaphysically discourteous to slight her."[12] Schnier's professional status has also been seriously affected by his personal crisis, and the novel describes him at the end of his rope, reconsidering his life in a lonely apartment, and calling acquaintances on the telephone for consolation or help. The telephone calls are constantly interspersed with his memories and serve the same function as the letters in *Herzog*. Schnier's comments bring out and expose the cultural, religious, and political hypocrisy of contemporary German life. They are witty and pungent, thought-provoking, bitter, and ironic, yet they lack the intensity, penetration, and urgency of most of Herzog's asides and jottings. The techniques used by Bellow are complexly related to his intention of dramatising the comic aspects of Herzog's crisis. In *The Clown* the main devices are flashback and irony, and the manner of their employment is conventional and stereotyped. They fall short in trying to achieve a close approximation of the protagonist's troubled state of mind because their situational placement is not determined with the kind of imaginative perspective that gives order and depth in *Herzog* to, say, the courtroom scenes or the memories of the "ancient times."

Also, in the resolution of Schnier's crisis, *The Clown* seems to fit a little too snugly in the pattern of the usual modern confessional novel. Schnier rejects the roles necessary for success and chooses to be himself by accepting his *real* situation in life. He decides to beg by singing because there is nothing else left for him to do: that, for him, is the end of his tether, the farthest limit to which his failure can take him. He is, therefore, the typical confessional hero who, in Peter M. Axthelm's words, explores his being "not in an effort to move closer to God, but in a quest for a meaning which does not depend on God or on any force outside the self."[16]

Herzog also chooses to be what he is, but his affirmation is moderated by his need to relate himself significantly, and unlike the confessional hero, to an external referent—God and other human beings—because he has learnt from experience that a reliance on the self to the exclusion of everything else can be dangerous and nerve-wrecking. Herzog's stand appears more credible because he has experienced the full range of feelings that go in the making of a man. He has been alienated and swayed by pride and evil, he has suffered and known the futility of anguish, and he has finally seen the sublimation of his experiences into a system of ethical values. He is a moral survivor and his options are on the side of life: he has chosen joy for suffering, togetherness for alienation, humility for pride, and God for monstrous subjectivity. At the close of the novel he is still groping toward a life stabilised by the values he holds precious, but his clairvoyance assures the reader that he is on the right track. In the case of Boll's hero, on the other hand, one is legitimately inclined to ask: *After begging, what*?

MR. SAMMLER'S PLANET

"One wants from Bellow a novel," wrote Irving Howe in his review of *Herzog*, "that will not be confined to a single besieged consciousness but instead will negotiate the kind of leap into the world which he proclaims, to savour the world's freshness and struggle against its recalcitrance..."[1] The novel that followed *Herzog* did not fulfil, to the letter, Howe's expectations, but it did spell out, through its structure and content, Bellow's preoccupation with the problems that could seriously limit the kind of affirmation Howe had demanded. *Mr. Sammler's Planet* functions, contrary to Howe's hopes, within the enclosure of a single consciousness: Bellow brings the third person point of view so close to the first person that the two are almost united in communicating the flow of the protagonist's consciousness. The blending of the protagonist's perceptions of external reality with his inner, subjective processes results in a monologue that virtually *becomes* the novel. To Bellow:

> It is hard work, a book like that. Each word is very carefully weighed and connected, closely connected, to the man. The internal processes of Mr. Sammler require the very narrowest attention. You have to see that he is never speaking out of character and that he never says anything simply

for the sake of saying the thing, but what I wanted to create —I don't know how successful I was in this—was the thinking of such a person, never disconnecting the thought from the person, so that these things are not presented in the book as sermons, but rather as a monologue.[2]

The extended use of the monologue necessarily leads to a preponderance of ideas. It would, however, be incorrect to argue, as Keith Opdahl does, that the ideas in *Mr. Sammler's Planet* "overshadow the tale,"[3] for, strictly speaking, the tale and the ideas in the novel are not mutually exclusive. Since the movement of the plot closely follows the movement of ideas, the book's power to grip the reader depends chiefly on the excitement generated by the ideas themselves. Whatever plot there is consists of experiences and encounters in the life of an old man who draws from them material for his reflections on life. To Bellow, "these thoughts are so intimately embedded in the mind of Mr. Sammler and are so much a part of his subjective state" that they should not be regarded as "mere exercises in thought."[4] Sammler is employed primarily as a symbolic observer because his age, intellectual sophistication, foreignness, and uprightness help to accentuate Bellow's indictment of contemporary American Society. Like the old man in Yeats' "Sailing to Byzantium," Sammler—a widower of seventy-plus, one time friend of H.G. Wells, himself steeped in the history of ideas, wounded in one eye by the brutalities inflicted during the Nazi occupation of Poland, and now living in a West side New York apartment with his niece in the financial security provided by his rich nephew Dr. Gruner—is, at first sight, "a tattered coat upon a stick."[5] There is much around him that appears disagreeable, much that makes him feel different "from the rest of the species" (p. 43), yet deep within he has a reservoir of vitality which enables him to assume mature and dignified stances of dissent. The choice of such a hero has the obvious advantage of moral and esthetic distancing, and, by a perfect synchronization of the third and first person points of view, Bellow defines Sammler's persona and conveys through it provocative and disturbing reflections on the nature of life in the late nineteen sixties:

If the majority walked about as if under a spell, sleepwalkers, circumscribed by, in the grip of, minor neurotic trifling aims, individuals like Sammler were only one stage forward, awakened not to purpose but to aesthetic consumption of the environment. Even if insulted, pained, somewhere bleeding, not broadly expressing any anger, not crying out with sadness, but translating heartache into delicate, even piercing observation (p. 44).

The unpleasant incident that mars Sammler's lecture at Columbia University offers a striking illustration of his ability to transmute personal experience into generalised sociological insights. Shouted down in obscene language by a student activist in the middle of his lecture, Sammler is not so much personally aggrieved as struck by the will of the young to offend. "The worst of it," he feels, "from the point of view of the young people themselves, was that they acted without dignity. They had no view of the nobility of being intellectuals and judges of the social order" (p. 45). Bellow artfully suggests the contrast between the rational, and increasingly weakening, attitudes of social order and the irrational and criminal forces of disruption in Sammler's encounter with a black whom he observes picking pockets in a bus. The Negro pursues him and threatens him by exposing his genitalia. Sammler is so fascinated by the confident and "serenely masterful" expression on the criminal's face and the "mystifying certitude" with which he displays himself that he submits to the threat in silence and is reluctant to discuss the event with anyone (p. 50). Later, when, at his instance, his son-in-law intervenes in a fight between the pickpocket and Feffer, an acquaintance, and knocks the black down, Sammler is horrified. He considers the act inhuman (it recalls the painful moment of his own eye being smashed by a riflebutt in Poland) and against the "idea of noblesse" which, he believes, the black man embodies. His ambivalent attitude towards the pickpocket—his earlier unsuccessful attempt to report him to the police and his subsequent pity for him—brings out the coexistence of civic and human qualities in his personality and his admiration for what, in his view, constitutes a silencing proof of life.

Bellow further establishes Sammler's distance from his

environment by setting him against several younger individuals who are contemporary in a sense in which he is not. Each of these characters represents a ruling passion or a drive—relating to intellectual sensibility, crime, sex, or art—the insane pursuit of which renders him or her inauthentic and comical. Margotte, Sammler's widowed niece, is forever discussing current intellectual cliches (such as Hannah Arendt's phrase, "The Banality of Evil"), but her foothold on ordinary life is so weak that she cannot even "wash a tomato without getting her sleeves wet" (p. 17). Shula, his daughter, steals the manuscript of Govinda Lal on lunar habitation to keep him supplied with the latest ideas on his once contemplated but now virtually abandoned memoir of H.G. Wells. Sammler reflects that by stealing his daughter became 'contemporary—lawless. She was experiencing the Age" (p. 162). If his nephew's daughter Angela is for endless variety in sex Walter Bruch, Margotte's cousin, is unable to overcome his fetish for female arms. Modern Art is the obsession of Sammler's psychopathic son-in-law Eisen, who paints like "a little schoolgirl learning to draw pretty people, with cupid mouths and long eyelashes" (p. 65). Angela's brother Wallace is so distracted that he tries to be *nearly* everything— lawyer, physicist, mathematician, Ph.D. in behaviourial science, pilot, alcoholic, and homosexual, with interests ranging from racecourse gambling and baseball to aerial photography. Sammler is conscious that the inauthenticity of these individuals is the result of their desire to mythologize themselves in their revulsion from ordinary life. The basic impulse behind this desire is the terror of death: "at the present level of crude vision," Sammler discerns, "agitated spirits fled from the oppressiveness of 'the common life,' separating themselves from the rest of their species, from the life of their species, hoping perhaps to get away (in some peculiar sense) from the death of their species" (p. 147). Sammler examines his contemporaries and discovers that in seeking originality they have merely become derivative: "And of what—of Paiutes, of Fidel Castro ? No, of Hollywood extras" (p. 149). Since greatness is inconceivable without models, Sammler realises that it is better to "accept the inevitability of imitation and then to imitate good things" (p. 149). But this would be possible only if man gives up his claim on permanence and personal myth and seeks reconciliation with intermediacy and representation—"Otherwise the individual must be the failure he now sees and knows himself to be" (p. 149).

Sammler finds in Elya Gruner, his rich nephew and benefactor, the dignity and sanity he considers singularly absent in the younger people around him and their prototypes in society. Gruner's approaching death from aneurysm provides the motivation for much of Sammler's speculations about the meaning of a fulfilled life in a dishevelled society. Gruner's self restraint, his calm acceptance of his fatal ailment, and his willingness to live the last few days of his life with equanimity, as if it is a part of an assignment he is obligated to fulfil under contract, suggest his attachment to a system of values cherished by Sammler but alien to his contemporaries whose great anxiety to escape death is manifested in their desire to abandon the earth for the moon. It would be incorrect to assume that Sammler idealises Gruner. On the contrary, the obvious defects of Gruner's character—vanity, pride, boastfulness, contacts with the Mafia, and touchiness—are not lost on him (p. 303). But the basic stability of Gruner's character and his genuine concern for others seem to render these defects negligible. Gruner, like Sammler, has accepted the finitude and ordinariness of earthly life and has found peace with the fear of mortality and intermediacy: "if the earth deserves to be abandoned, if we are now to be driven streaming into other world, starting with the moon, it is not because of the likes of you, Sammler would have said." (p. 86).

In its search for the sources of stability and meaning in a society unsure of its moral direction, *Mr. Sammler's Planet* is as much about Sammler as about the planet he inhabits. Sammler regards the earth as *his* planet despite the conditions that disrupt normal life and seeks to affirm human existence at a time when mankind is almost on the verge of exploring the possibility of creating a new world on the moon. In affirming life on the earth, Sammler is torn by two opposite pressures: he is alive to the fact that the advances in technology have not at all resolved the maddening conditions of human life, but he also knows that there is as yet no adequate substitute for what the earth offers. His affirmation is, therefore, necessarily marginal and agonized as it is open to the spirit of doubt that invariably accompanies a regard for truth; at the same time, it steers clear of the stereotyped stances that tend to formulate life and reality within the fixities of a pre-determined logic. Sammler rejects the millenialist point of view—typified by his grandniece Angela—which holds that the paradise is now and can be realised through instant and ecstatic self-gratification. The life-style of the flower generation does not also appear to him because it misconstrues the "real purpose of civilization" by glorifying "neolithic life in an automated society" (p. 227). His knowledge of the evil present in the world prevents him from savouring its freshness and celebrating its glory. Still, he is doubtful of the assurance of the eschatological stance which assumes that doom is certain. In such matters he is unable to take a decisive either/or stand because he knows, like Herzog, that intellectual attempts to make sweeping historical judgments are, by their nature, hollow and untrue. As such, he has only honest doubts, no forced convictions. Robbed, thus, of the certainties that result from a blind commitment to ideology, he is content to limit his affirmation to the notion of the sacredness of life and to the preservation of this notion through a personal ethic sustained by "the sense of God" (p. 236). "As long as there is no ethical life," he asserts, "and everything is poured so barbarously and recklessly into personal gesture this (suffering) must be endured" (p. 235).

Sammler's personal ethic finds its clearest articulation in his dialogue with Dr. Govinda Lal, an Indian biophysicist, on the desirability of human settlement on the moon. Although the dialogue occupies one-eighth of the total print-space of the novel and provokes the reader to raise vital questions about its own structural and ideational justification, it is surprising that critics and reviewers have not so far accorded it the attention it really deserves. The reviews in *The Times Literary Supplement*,[6] *Saturday Review*,[7] and *New York Times Books Review*[8] ignore altogether any consideration of the dialogue. Critics such as Edward Grossman,[9] Keith Opdahl,[10] and John J. Clayton[11] are so exclusively concerned with an evaluation of Bellow's motives in *Mr. Sammler's Planet* that they are able to devote very little consideration to the moon-dialogue. The general critical indifference to the moon-dialogue makes it necessary that its affinity with Bellow's method be established and its organic relationship with the novel brought into proper perspective before a study of the conceptual framework of Sammler's ethic is undertaken.

It ought to be recalled that long discussions and dialogues have always been essential constituents of all of Bellow's novels. Joseph converses at length with the Spirit of Alternatives in *Dangling Man*, Asa Leventhal with old Schlossberg in *The Victim*, Tommy Wilhelm with Dr. Tamkin in *Seize the Day*, Henderson with King Dahfu in *Henderson the Rain King*, and Citrine with Humboldt in *Humboldt's Gift*. In *Augie March*, the hero, conscious of the necessity of striking a balance with the "axial lines" of life, has a hard time with people who are eager to convert him to their view of reality. And although in *Herzog* the hero's attitude to his Reality Instructors is essentially negative, he does try to communicate with a large number of people—intellectuals, philosophers, politicians, men who matter and those who don't—by reacting through his remarks, thinking, jottings, and letters to their opinions and viewpoints. The dialogue is usually held with people who are older than the hero, presumably superior and mature in that they have extracted a philosophy out of their experience of life, and of considerable mental agility. The Bellow hero is never fully persuaded by his Reality Instructors: the dialogue may help him develop an insight into his own situation (*DM, TV, HRK, H, HG*), indicate points of departure (*AM, H, HG*), or cheat him completely (*SD*), but almost invariably it offers the hero an opportunity to encounter versions of reality and to see that reality far outmatches the constructions imposed on it by the human mind. The ideas generated by the dialogues are always, therefore, integral to the hero's experience and his quest for meaning: they are a part of the total scheme of the novel and cannot be conceived of as a mere padding of thought on a skimpy plot.

That the moon-dialogue grows organically out of the narrative of *Mr. Sammler's Planet* and is not imposed upon it can be shown by an attentive reading of the novel. After Shula, Sammler's half-crazy daughter, steals Dr. Lal's notebook *The Future of the Moon* to help her father write his memoir of

H.G. Wells, the meeting between Sammler and Lal, if not the dialogue, can be anticipated. The opening sentence of the manuscript—"How long will this earth remain the only home of man?" (p. 51)—triggers speculation in Sammler's mind on the prospect of creating living conditions on the moon and the future of the earth. He himself realises that his musings—which range from pure futurological wonder at the changes called for in man's behaviour by his new "lunar conditions" to a feeling of regret and loss at what the earth, with "its white and its blue, its fleeces, the great glitter afloat," is going to become—are a preparation to meet Dr. Lal (pp. 134-135). Sammler's conversation with Wallace, his nephew's son who has signed up with Pan Am for a possible moon-trip in the future, provokes more thought on the subject and almost forestalls his stance in the oncoming dialogue. Wallace wonders why a person like Sammler "wouldn't be raring to go" (p. 183). Sammler replies that he feels little craving to undertake the journey; the reasons he offers stem from the terms he has reached with life *here*:

"To the moon? But I don't even want to go to Europe," Mr. Sammler said, "Besides, if I had my choice, I'd prefer the ocean bottom... I seem to be a depth man rather than height man. I do not personally care for the illimitable. The ocean, however deep, has a top and a bottom, whereas there is no sky ceiling... Personally I require a ceiling, although a high one (pp. 183-184).

But Wallace, continuously distracted in search of the unusual and the different, is much too feeble intellectually to play to Sammler the role of either a Reality Instructor or even an intelligent dissenter. Other people who surround Sammler—Angela, Walter Bruch, Shula, and Margotte—also fail to assume such a role. They are culture enthusiasts and faddists, lacking a dignity and discipline of the mind that would meet Sammler's approval. Even Govinda Lal is not accepted with any enthusiasm in the beginning. Sammler is impressed by the intelligence and quality displayed in the notebook *The Future of the Moon*, but he has to overcome several personal prejudices before he can bring himself to converse with Lal. The prejudices are mostly temperamental and range from uneasiness with

Lal's "formal Edwardian pedantic Hindu English" to his supposedly excitable Indian temperament. And even when Lal's presence renders such reservations unnecessary, the approval granted him is only provisional. It is later in conversation that Sammler discovers his fondness for Lal: "this Lal was like Ussher Arkin, a man he could talk to" (p. 211). Also, obliquely stated in the text are several references that point to common elements in their intellectual orientation. First, both are outsiders to America, having left behind strong traditional and cultural roots; both are, therefore, equally fascinated and intrigued by the variety and excitement of contemporary American life and its almost exotic quality. To Sammler, "New York was getting worse than Naples or Salonika... You opened a jeweled door into degradation, from hypercivilized Byzantine luxury straight into the state of nature" (p. 71). Lal also confesses to experiencing similar feelings when he first visited the United States (p. 204). Second, both share a past of mass-killings: Sammler has been a victim of the cruelties inflicted on the Jews in Poland; Lal has been through the horror of communal violence in Calcutta in 1947. Their experience of violence and human misery has made it imperative that their concern for the future of mankind be more than theoretical. And, finally, in his preoccupation with the ideas contained in Lal's notebook, Sammler feels so close to the Indian scientist that he is momentarily led to believe that the Jews are essentially Asians: "he himself, a jew, no matter how Britanicized or Americanized, was also an Asian" (p. 116).

But, in spite of the background they emotionally share, Sammler and Lal have moved over to different standpoints of belief. Sammler has given up the intellectual culture he once savoured in favour of religion. Tired of Marx, Weber, Scheler, Oppenheimer, Adorno, Marcuse, Brown, Ortega, and Valery, he now reads only Meister Eckhardt and the Bible (p. 37). Lal's view of life has been shaped, on the one hand, by the biological sciences, and, on the other, by an imagination rooted in technology but almost poetic in character (p. 216). Born in a country of vast multitudes, he finds little wrong when the possibilities of space-research make human beings feel "that the intellectual power and skill of their own species opens the way" (p. 219). The conquest of the moon, he believes, is a "rational necessity" which, if ignored, might cause great dissatisfaction among human beings and ultimately lead to a death-wish: "If we could soar on and did not, we would condemn ourselves.... As it is, the species is eating itself up.... Much better the moon" (p. 219).

The Indian scientist's faith in the "rational necessity" of undertaking the moon-voyage is, however, undercut by an irony of which he is unaware himself. He is a romantic and makes a virtue of romantic irresponsibility by trying to disguise it in the value-free grammar of the biological sciences. He disagrees with Sammler that the talk of death-wish may be just rhetorical and that an implicit morality characterises the will to live and perform one's duty. "There is no duty in biology," Lal contends, "There is no sovereign obligation to one's breed. When biological destiny is fulfilled in reproduction the desire is often to die. We please ourselves in extracting ideas of duty from biology. But duty is pain. Duty is hateful—misery, oppressive" (p. 220).

Sammler is quick to perceive the fallacy in Lal's argument, and, though he is charmed by the Indian, he cannot help picturing him as a Faustian caricature "mentally rebounding from limits like a horsefly from glass" (p. 223). Taking up an orthodox stance against Lal's argument, Sammler asserts that the desire to abandon the earth for the moon can hardly be called rational. For if "it were a rational matter, then it would be rational to have justice on this planet first" (p. 237). The voyage to the moon is symptomatic of man's eternal hunger for the illimitable, a hunger that has always brought anguish and misery in its wake. Basic problems will not be resolved on another planet because human dissatisfaction may assume more intense forms there. Death-wish, therefore, is not the ultimate aspiration of man's biological destiny: it is an unnatural and abnormal craving, a denial of the powers of creation. He contests Lal's assertion that duty is painful, repressive, and abhorrent: ' being born one... obeys the will of God—with whatever inner reservations truth imposes" (p. 220). Duty may be painful, but it inculcates uprightness, "and this uprightness is no negligible thing" (p. 220).

Cognizance and acceptance of limits, to Sammler, are essential conditions for living without dissatisfaction or excessive desires. He traces the origin of the widespread discontent in our time to the history of the rise of individualism in the western world (p. 238). Conscious of his uniqueness, the individual desires to excel, lead an *interesting* life, be different from others: in consequence, he seeks "all other states of being in a diffused state of consciousness, not wishing to be any given thing but instead to become comprehensive, entering and leaving at will" (p. 235). Frustration in this endeavour leads to disillusionment, inauthenticity, and death-wish.

As obsession with uniqueness also conditions man to an inherently subjective view of reality. Ignoring the possibilities of existence in bone and blood, he begins to believe that only that which can be apprehended through his theoretical formulations is valid and meaningful. Thus, the knowledge which really matters and is innate to the soul is lost. The soul's "natural knowledge" is that there is "something in him (man) .... that deserves to go on" (pp. 235-236). Sammler believes that this instinct is inseparable from the "sense of God" which persists in spite of man's attempt to reason life away.

But how can the human soul be imbued with the "sense of God"? "Is God only the gossip of the living?" Sammler asks, questioning Lal's irreligious view of life (p. 236). The inability to decode the unknown often leads to disbelief. Man finds it hard to acknowledge that everything cannot be known. But once the mystery is accepted, Sammler feels, the recognition of life's contradictions, of what is mundane but truly human, of the affectations resulting from "need, affection, and love" (p. 236) necessarily follows. In such a state, "having set its relations with the infinite" and "entirely at home in the finite," man, like Kierkegaard's *real prodigy*, will be able "to carry the jewel of faith, making the motions of the infinite, and, as a result, needing nothing but the finite and the usual" (p. 62). Rejecting, thus, the deterministic influence of biological order on existence, Sammler makes a plea for "some order within," which he considers akin to love (p. 228). Such a perception makes it possible for him to affirm life *here*, in its finitude and commonness, and live relatedly in the present. Having found peace within himself on this planet he has no need to seek a better life on the moon. "The best I have found," he says, "is to be disinterested. Not as misanthropes dissociate themselves, by judging, but by not judging. By willing as God wills." (p. 236).

The incident that concludes the dialogue seems to have been intended by Bellow to fulfil a comic and symbolic function. Wallace's attempt to find his father's hidden wealth in the waterpipes misfires, and, as a result, the whole house is flooded. Sammler and Lal immediately suspend their discussion and, with the help of Shula, Margotte, and Wallace, try to bring the situation under control. The comic, anticlimactic interruption—a kind of mock apocalypse—obviously provides a foil to the seriousness with which the moon-voyage is debated between Sammler and Lal, enabling the reader to see the author's ambivalence toward the ideas proposed in the dialogue. At the symbolic level the interlude seems to suggest that serious discussions among intellectuals on the future of the earth are of no avail because the very possibility of human life can be put into jeopardy at any time by vested interests. It is with reference to such a context that Sammler's plea for an ethical life acquires its poignancy and relevance. Unless ethical imperatives are imbibed into feeling and conduct, life is reduced to mere biological phenomenon, emptied of the human, and subject to the laws that govern all biological phenomenon. The moon-dialogue presents Sammler's ethic in its rightful background and forms the core of the novel. A clear understanding of its structural and ideational relevance, therefore, affords a better approach to *Mr. Sammler's Planet* and enlarges the possibilities of appreciation.

Artur Sammler is the first of Bellow's heroes to forge a viable connexion with the world and affirm it through a personal ethic sanctified by a faith in God. Like Herzog, he is critical of "the modern religion of empty categories and the people who make the motions of knowledge" (p. 226), but he goes beyond Herzog's initial steps toward comprehension to achieve a clarity and authority of vision unavailable to Bellow's other heroes. It would be wrong to assume that *Mr. Sammler's Planet*, with its unmistakably positive, though agonized, affirmative tone marks a radical departure in Bellow's growth as a novelist. To say this is not to undermine the importance of the novel but to review the nature of its relationship with the preceding novels. In truth, *Mr. Sammler's Planet* represents a development rather than a difference, for many of the ideas projected in it are to be found in Bellow's earlier fiction. Bellow's comic treatment of people driven by obsessions to achieve a unique, personal destiny, his distrust of explanations of reality, and his faith in love and ordinary life are as much integral constituents of his earlier novels as of *Mr. Sammler's Planet*. Even the religious inclinations that underlie Sammler's ethic, with the allied virtues of duty, disinterestedness, and civility, are in a measure refined out of Herzog's experience. For a fuller appreciation of *Mr. Sammler's Planet* it is not so necessary to dwell on these aspects as to perceive how the earlier Bellow heroes have aged into Sammler and to comprehend the development that this maturation has brought about in Bellow's career as a novelist.

The distance between Sammler, who has sensed the presence of God, and Joseph, who considered God anterior, has not been covered by a sudden leap of faith. The limits set by Bellow on his mode of affirmation renders such a leap impossible, but from the fleeting glimpses of Sammler's past made available to the reader it is possible to detect in Sammler's background the familiar Bellow hero. To take an example, one can trace in Sammler's childhood habits the seeds of a malady common to all Bellow heroes—the desire to be exceptional and exclusive: "He was an only son spoiled by a mother who had herself been a spoiled daughter. An amusing recollection: When Sammler was a little boy he had covered his mouth, when he coughed, with the servant's hand to avoid getting germs on his hands" (pp. 60-61). The immediate referent to young Sammler's infantile attitude is suggested by Herozg's recall of an incident of his childhood illustrating how he too was spoiled by his mother :

She certainly spoiled me. Once, at nightfall, she was pulling me on the sled, over crusty ice, the tiny glitter of snow, perhaps four o'clock of a short day in January. Near the grocery we met an old baba in a shawl who said, "Why are you pulling him, daughter !" . . . "Daughter, don't sacrifice your strength to children," said the shawled crone in the freezing dusk of the street. I wouldn't get off the sled. I pretended not to understand (*H*, p. 139).

Herzog's insufficient understanding of life's truth is responsible for his attempt in early youth to seek reality not in the world around him but in the abstractions contained in books such as *The Decline of the West* and *The World as Will and Idea*. Bellow invokes the image of Sammler in early youth trying to become as Englishman and points out that the haughtiness and eccentricity cultivated by him were typical of an aristocracy divorced from real life :

> Then, when he was older, his mother herself... used to bring lean, nervous young Sammler his chocolate and croissants as he sat in his room reading Trollope and Bagehot, making an "Englishman" of himself. He and his mother had a reputation for eccentricity, irritability in those days. Not compassionate people. Not easily pleased. Haughty (p. 61).

Sammler's subsequent association with H. G. Wells—a Reality Instructor with cosmic fantasies—and the Bloomsbury group signifies his desire to seek a special personal destiny by becoming "an Anglophile intellectual polish Jew and person of culture" (p. 303). In this respect, he is little different from Wilhelm who ignored the truth about himself and hankered after a career in films, Augie who was keen on an independent fate, and Henderson who went to Africa to answer his spirit's troubled calling. The correction of Sammler's earlier naivety and his increased humanity result from his exposure to a reality not restricted, as in the previous novels, to a personal crisis concerning the fate of a single individual. The insane violence that trapped Sammler in Poland was directed against a whole race : it diffused "bad information about the very essence of being" (p. 90) and, in the inhumanity and indignity it induced, it levelled up commoners as well as aristocrats brought up on genteel ideas of privilege. Such an experience involved the death of a self whose presumptions had guided Sammler's early years in Poland :

> So, for his part, it had happened that Sammler, with his

wife and others, on a perfectly clear day, had had to strip naked. Waiting, then to be shot in the mass grave.... Sammler had already that day been struck in the eye by a gun butt and blinded. In contraction from life, when naked, he already felt himself dead (p. 137).

The reader is informed that at that time Sammler had no God and "For many years, in his own mind, there was no judge but himself" (p. 141). The sheer necessity of survival, Bellow suggests, compelled Sammler to overcome his self-centeredness and "turn to the external world for curious ciphers and portents" (p. 89). Hidden in a mausoleum and saved by the caretaker of the cemetery, Sammler discovered that "a straw or a spider thread or a stain, a beetle or a sparrow had to be interpreted. Symbols everywhere, and metaphysical messages" (p. 90). Like Asa Leventhal and Herzog, whose sensibility acquired refinement after a recognition of the possibility of vice within themselves, Sammler arrived at a consciousness of his propensity to evil in the murder he committed of a German straggler. By vividly retaining in his later years the memory of the event and of the thrill it brought him (pp. 140-141), Sammler affirms his creatureliness and acknowledges the fact that even at the cost of doing something irreversible he was forced to enter into a relationship with his quarry, another human being. The persistent nature of the memory suggests Sammler's acceptance within himself of the elements that represent the darker impulses of his soul and define the limits of his humanity.

Sammler's traumatic experience of the atrocities in Poland incapacitated him emotionally to such an extent that "For quite a long time he had felt that he was not necessarily human" (p. 117). He became disaffected, uninterested in others, and indifferent even to the thought of his own recovery. Bellow intimates that Sammler's return to normalcy followed several years after the war through a contact with mundane and ordinary reality: "In the human setting, alongwith everyone else, among particulars of ordinary life he *was* human—and, in short, creatureliness crept in again" (p. 117). It is, therefore, no accident that in his dialogue with Govinda Lal, Sammler offers a forceful defence of creatureliness, ordinary life, and the virtues of duty and disinterestedness.

The essential experience of Sammler, it will be seen, is not unlike the experience of Bellow's other heroes. But what is more important is the inference that the nobility so visibly present in him is the result of the cultivation of insights gained from his essential experience. It is also possible to imply, in retrospect, that the possibilities affirmed in the novels preceeding *Mr. Sammler's Planet* suggest a direction of moral growth which lead to the figure of Sammler. By portraying a hero of Sammler's age and stature, Bellow has obviously overcome his confessed inability to "justify the virtue of the virtuous."[12] Bellow, like other modern writers, found it difficult to show goodness as fully developed because of a literary prejudice that specialised in being "realistic" about virtue and considered it necessary to expose the hypocrisy motivated and pretended goodness.[13] The development *Mr. Sammler's Planet* marks over the rest of Bellow's fiction has to be located in the precarious combination of intelligence and kindliness in the character of Sammler—a combination rarely discernible in the literature of the last hundred years.[14] Such a combination makes it possible for him to balance his skepticism toward the cliches of "unrealistic" affirmation with his preference for discipline in conduct and thought (p. 136). His trust in virtue can withstand the onslaught of doubt because it is born out of an instinctive knowledge that human life on earth is under a contract to aspire to a measure of significance before death takes its toll: "The terms which in his inmost heart each man knows. As I know mine" (p. 313). As a result, the inevitability of death does not spur Sammler to seek the essence of life in supposedly exciting adventures; rather, he considers death as a moment of honour to an individual alive to his sense of duty, an occasion of release "from the bondage of the ordinary and the finite... from Nature, from impressions, and from everyday life" (p. 117).

Paul Tillich's[15] analysis of the interrelationship of faith and courage provides a suitable context for discussing Sammler's affirmation of the possibilities of a virtuous and disciplined life *in spite of* the presence of evil and the terror of death. Tillich defines faith as the experience of the power of being that makes self-affirmation possible in spite of the threat of non-being.[16] "Faith accepts in spite of," says Tillich, "and out of the 'in spite of' of faith the 'in spite of' of courage is born."[17] The courage of conduct and conviction that Sammler brings to his personal ethic grows out of his faith in God, or, to employ Tillich's categories, in "the power of being which transcends everything that is and in which everything that is participates."[18] The two important choices that Sammler makes at the time of Gruner's death are dictated by his courage and lend him a heroic stature unapproached by any of the protagonists of Bellow's earlier fiction. His refusal to intercede on Angela's behalf is motivated by his desire to remain disinterested and non-judging; at the same time, Angela's unwillingness to make some sign of reconciliation to her dying father provokes him to confront her with the blunt truth about herself even though he knows that unfriendly relations with her may considerably affect his financial security in the future (p. 306). He also dissuades his daughter Shula from appropriating the illicit wealth she finds in the Gruner estate and chooses to remain content with "what there is" in case Gruner, failing to provide for him, leaves him at Angela's mercy (pp. 308-310). He is firm in his resolve that "under no circumstances and on no account would he become involved in a perverse relationship with Angela in which he had to listen for his supper" (p.160). His consolation lies in the humble prayer of Meister Eckhardt which, in its applicability to people in his situation, restates his own faith and courage: "as long as creatures comfort and are able to comfort you, you will never find true comfort. But if nothing can comfort you save God, truly God will console you" (p. 253).

In *Mr. Sammler's Planet* Bellow makes no attempt to take shelter in a protective aestheticism: he places the novel on the crosswire of contemporary history to highlight Sammler's desperate search for a rationale of living on the earth at a time when most people regard the moon as a possible habitat of escape. The novel is his answer to the really powerful men in our society who hold writers and poets in contempt "because they get no evidence from modern literature that anybody is thinking about any significant question."[19] Bellow's intense concern with significant questions leads him to fulfil, in *Mr. Sammler's Planet*, the two aims of ar the holds precious : art, he believes, "must be understood as a purgation of consciousness"[20] and "has something to do with the achievement of stillness in the midst of chaos."[21] Sammler, like Herzog, rejects the reductive processes of intellection that corrupt consciousness and, in so doing, reaches over, more firmly and securely than Herzog, to a centre of faith that promises a meaningful existence through the limits it imposes on thought and conduct. Sammler may not have negotiated an ecstatic leap into the world, but his commitment to life is more authentic than that of the "princes of the big time . . . who whoop it up for life"[22] and is, consequently, more acceptable.

CONCLUSION
Toward a Mystique of Saul Bellow

Discussing recent responses to the problem of selfhood in *Sincerity and Authenticity,* Lionel Trilling regretfully notes the tendency of distinguished contemporary thinkers like R.D. Laing, Norman O. Brown, and M. Foucault to regard insanity as "a state of being in which an especially high degree of authenticity inheres."[1] Such a view gains support and weight, in Trilling's opinion, from two interdependent assumptions. The first rests on the argument that insanity is governed by its own rationale and entails a "direct and appropriate" criticism and rejection of the "coercive inauthenticity of society."[2] The second defines insanity as a "negation of limiting conditions in general, a form of personal existence in which power is assured by self-sufficiency."[3] Trilling believes that the currency of these dubious assumptions is the result of a hypocrisy "characteristic of the intellectual life of our culture"[4] because:

> ... we must yet take it to be significant of our circumstance that many among us find it gratifying to entertain the thought that alienation is to be overcome only by the completeness of alienation, and that alienation completed is not a deprivation or deficiency but a potency. Perhaps exactly because the thought is assented to so facilely, so without what used to be called seriousness, it might seem that no expression of disaffection from the social existence was ever so desperate as this eagerness to say that authenticity

of personal being is achieved through an ultimate isolateness and through the power that this is presumed to bring.[5]

Trilling's dismayed reaction to the uncertain and imbalanced moral priorities of our time provides a suitable context for summarising the affirmative imperatives of Bellow's novels. Bellow, no less than Trilling, is concerned with the problem of moral and intellectual health, and his novels give evidence of his anxiety to arrive at an understanding of the norms that may restore normalcy and stability to the individual. He believes that refined forms of individuality can be approximated by liberating the soul from the inauthenticity in which it is trapped by its adherence to the cult of the ego. The cult of the ego discards ordinariness and exaggerates the capacity of the self to achieve meaning through an intense pursuit of experience: it encourages paranoiac feelings of self-sufficiency and ultimately induces the kind of mistaken and insane trust in alienation that invites Trilling's censure in *Sincerity and Authenticity*. Bellow shows through the instances of his protagonists that egocentricity can be cured and normalcy restored by an acceptance of ordinariness and a recognition of the intuitions of one's significance. The sublimation of the protagonist's consciousness inspires a more accommodative attitude toward others, awakens a sharper perception of the drives that govern the human personality, and instils a willingness to obey the norms of ethical and prosocial conduct: it signifies, in effect, his openness to faith. Faith, in Bellow's scheme, is measured by an individual's capacity to enter the whole reality with a state of mind unencumbered by pretentious concepts of the nature and purpose of life. It originates in the protagonist's preoccupation with his own significance and refers human action to a region of experience where all values are centered. The religious temper, as opposed to the neurotic temper, is relaxed in paradoxes and does not react against the limiting conditions of the environment with insane anger. It accepts reality in its intricate variety and rejoices in the richness of the created world. In its tolerant view of imperfections and contradictions, it displays an intimate nearness with the comic imagination. It mocks and laughs away solemn pronouncements about the nature of life so that a more reasoned comprehension of an individual's significance may be possible.

The affirmative tones that become increasingly clear and prominent in Bellow's later novels give expression to his conviction that a novelist must go beyond the simplistic categories of optimism and pessimism, hope and despair, togetherness and alienation, and explore reality with a strong regard for truth. He must not complacently accept fashionable critiques of society, but make his own investigations to arrive at an authenticated estimate of the human condition. It is true, Bellow says in his Nobel Lecture, that

> ... there is a violent uproar but we are not absolutely dominated by it. We are still able to think, to discriminate, and to feel. The purer, subtler, higher activities have not succumbed to fury or to nonsense. Not yet. Books continue to be written and read. It may be more difficult to reach the whirling mind of a modern reader but it is possible to cut through the noise and reach the quiet zone .... The unending cycle of crises that began with the First World War has formed a kind of person, one who has lived through terrible, strange things, and in whom there is an observable shrinkage of prejudices, a casting off of disappointing ideologies, an ability to live with many kinds of madness, an immense desire for certain durable human goods—truth, for instance, or freedom, or wisdom.[6]

In order to preserve this regard for truth in his novels, Bellow adopts a method suitable for communicating the mystique toward which his protagonists grope. However, he makes no attempt to turn his mystique into a cult for the redemption of the faithful because he seems to distrust all mystiques at the level of abstraction—even the one for which he indicates an unmistakable preference in his novels. An interesting illustration of this in-built skepticism of Bellow's method is his story "The Gonzaga Manuscripts" which brings into focus his assumed mockery of his own cherished modes of affirmation.[7] Clarence Feiler, a research scholar, is attached to the poetry of Manuel Gonzaga, a Spanish poet, whose philosophy of life appears suspiciously like Bellow's own. Feiler is so caught up in his feverish search for a lost manuscript of the poet that he forgets that he is turning into a complete antithesis of what Gonzaga stood for. He is moved, theoretically, by Gonzaga's affirmation of creatureliness, but in his day to day encounters he is unable to appreciate the creaturely instincts of others and considers them intolerable. The "moral" of the story is that even the best of mystiques can be debased and rendered ineffective when divorced from reality and idealised into an obsession. Since, as Eric Hoffer contends, the true believer in the chaos of modern society can only be a fanatic,[8] Bellow justifiably feels that "in an age of madness, to expect to be untouched by madness is a form of madness" and that "the pursuit of sanity can be a form of madness, too" (*HRK*, p. 25).

Bellow's use of Socratic irony reflects his anxiety to give credibility to his affirmation and to bring it within the realm of the possible. The irony confronts the protagonist with the error implicit in his way of life and suggests, through implication, the desirability of cultivating a changed or a more balanced outlook. Thus, Herzog realises that in seeking revenge on his divorced wife and her lover—in seeking justice—he had resorted to a greater anarchy than what he had condemned in existing social systems. "Social organization," he acknowledges, "for all its clumsiness and evil, has accomplished far more and embodies more good than I do, for at least it sometimes gives justice. I am a mess, and talk about justice" (*H*, p. 220). Sammler, in spite of his altruistic inclinations to "do something," is held in check by the sobering thought that "it is a dangerous illusion to think one can do much for more than a very few" (*SP*, p. 228). Evidently, Bellow maintains, unlike R.D. Laing, Norman O. Brown, M. Foucault, Norman Mailer, and Sylvia Plath, that a recognition of limits, of the errors of one's sensibility, and of the existence of an entity greater than oneself is a surer mark of authenticity than the inflation of the ego to a point where it begins to act as a counter-world. As case studies of the particular subtleties of particular crises, his novels significantly confront the problem of an individual's survival in modern society without the rhetoric of nihilism, "avoiding the absurdity of empty rebellion."[9] His belief that "There may be truths on the side of life" dissuades him from an uncritical acceptance of despair, alienation, and meaninglessness. "I'm not at all ready to stop hoping," he says, because "There may be some truths which are, after all, our friends in the universe."[10] To Bellow, such "friendly" universal truths are an integral part of the "natural knowledge" of the soul. They may be blurred temporarily by ignorance or evaded by explanations, but cannot be completely destroyed. Bellow's novels are dedicated to their rediscovery—to their anxious but tenacious affirmation in the lives of his protagonists.

Notes

INTRODUCTION : THE TERRITORY AHEAD

1. Chirantan Kulshrestha, "An Indian Writer Remembers Saul Bellow," *Span*, Vol. XIX, No. 2, February 1977, p. 32.
2. *Ibid.*
3. *Ibid.*
4. *Ibid.*
5. Chirantan Kulshrestha, "A Conversation with Saul Bellow," *Chicago Review*, Vol. 23, No. 4 & Vol. 24, No. 1, p. 14.
6. *Ibid.*, p. 14-15.
7. Saul Bellow, "A World Too Much With Us," *Critical Inquiry*, Autumn 1975, Vol. 2, No. 1, p. 9.
8. *Ibid.*
9. One thinks here mainly of John J. Clayton, *Saul Bellow : In Defense of Man* (Bloomington, 1971); Sarah Blacher Cohen, *Saul Bellow's Enigmatic Laughter* (Urbana, 1974); Brigitte Scheer-Schazler, *Saul Bellow* (New York, 1972); and Gilbert Porter, *Whence The Power ? The Artistry and Humanity of Saul Bellow* (Columbia, 1974).
10. Tony Tanner, *Saul Bellow* (Edinburgh, 1965), pp. 107-11.
11. Ray B. West, "Six American Authors in Search of a Hero," *Sewanee Review*, 65 (Summer, 1957), p. 505.
12. Leslie A. Fiedler, "Some Footnotes on the Fiction of '56," *The Reporter*, 15 (December 13, 1956), p. 46.
13. Helen Weinberg, *The New Novel in America : The Kafkan Mode in Contemporary Fiction* (Ithaca, 1970) p. 62.
14. "A Conversation with Saul Bellow," p. 12.
15. Allen Guttmann, *The Jewish Writer in America : Assimilation and the Crisis of Identity* (New York, 1971), pp. 178-221.
16. Irving Malin, *Saul Bellow's Fiction* (Carbondale, 196)), p. 46.
17. Robert Alter, *After the Tradition* (New York, 1969), p. 10.
18. "A Conversation with Saul Bellow," p. 13.
19. Harold Rosenberg, *Discovering the Present* (Chicago, 1973), p. 223.

CHAPTER 1

WRITING AS A MODE OF AFFIRMATION

1. Gustave Flaubert, *Letters*, ed. Richard Rumbold, trans. J.M. Cohen (London, 1950), pp. 106-110.
2. James Joyce, *A Portrait of the Artist as a Young Man* (New York, 1968), p. 215.
3. T.S. Eliot, *The Use of Poetry and the Use of Criticism* (London, 1930), p. 31.
4. Andre Gide, *The Counterfeiters* with *Journal* of "The Counterfeiters" trans. Dorothy Bussy (New York, 1927), pp. 171-177.
5. Erich Auerbach, *Mimesis* (New York, 1957), p. 487.
6. R.W.B. Lewis, *The Picaresque Saint* (Philadelphia, 1958), p. 19.
7. *Ibid.*, p. 21.
8. *The Picaresque Saint*, pp. 25-26.
9. *Ibid.*
10. Quoted in "A Conversation with Saul Bellow," p. 10.
11. *Ibid.*
12. Saul Bellow, "The Nobel Lecture," *The American Scholar*, Vol. 46, No. 3, Summer 1977, p. 321.
13. *Ibid.*, p. 12.
14. Saul Bellow, "Writers and Morals" Xerox copy of the original and as yet unpublished essay with Bellow's insertions, additions, and corrections in the margin and between the lines, *Series C, Box 2, Folder 8*, Saul Bellow Papers at the Joseph Regenstein Library, University of Chicago, pp. 5-6.
15. *Ibid.*
16. "Bellow on Himself and America," *Jerusalem Post Weekly*, July 6, 1970, No. 506, p. 10.
17. Writers and Morals," pp. 5-6.
18. *Ibid.*
19. *Ibid.*, p. 11.
20. Saul Bellow, "Distractions of a Fiction Writer," *The Living Novel*, ed. Granville Hicks (New York, 1962), p. 30.
21. "A Conversation with Saul Bellow," p. 11.
22. Gordon Lloyd Harper, "Saul Bellow : An Interview," *Paris Review*, 36 (Winter, 1966), pp. 65-66.
23. *Ibid.*, p. 57.
24. *Ibid.*, p. 58.
25. "Saul Bellow : An Interview," p. 58.
26. "Mystic Trade," Interview with Jim Douglas Henry published in *The Listener*, Vol. 81, No. 2095, May 22, 1969, p. 707.
27. "Bellow on Himself and America," *Jerusalem Post Weekly*, July 13, 1970, No. 507, p. 14 (Sequel to No. 506).
28. "The Writer as Moralist," *The Atlantic*, Vol. 211, No. 3, March 1963, p. 61.

NOTES

29. Harold Rosenberg, *The Anxious Object* (New York, 1969), p. 19.
30. *Ibid.*, pp. 19-20.
31. Lionel Trilling, *Sincerity and Authenticity* (Cambridge, Mass., 1973), p. 41.
32. *Ibid.*, p. 41-42.
33. "A Conversation with Saul Bellow," p. 11.
34. Saul Bellow, "The Thinking Man's Wasteland," *Saturday Review*, April 3, 1965, p. 20.
35. "The Writer as Moralist," p. 62.
36. *Ibid.*
37. Jane Howard, "Saul Bellow Considers His Planet," *Life*, Vol. 68, No. 12, April 3, 1970, p. 58.
38. Saul Bellow, "Two Faces for a Hostile World," rev. of Jean Dutourd's *Five A.M.*, *New York Times Book Review*, 61 (August 26, 1956), pp. 4-5.
39. "The Writer as Moralist," p. 62.
40. *Ibid.*
41. *Ibid.*
42. Saul Bellow, "The Uses of Adversity," *The Reporter*, 21 (October 1, 1959), pp. 42-44.
43. Saul Bellow, "The Sealed Treasure," *The Open Form*, ed. Alfred Kazin (New York, 1961), pp. 4-5.
44. *Ibid.*, pp. 5-6.
45. *Ibid.*
46. *Ibid.*
47. "Saul Bellow : An Interview," p. 67.
48. "A Conversation with Saul Bellow," p. 9.
49. "The Thinking Man's Wasteland," p. 20.
50. "The Sealed Treasure," p. 8.
51. Saul Bellow, "The Writer and the Audience," *Perspectives*, No. 9, Autumn 1954, p. 102.
52. "Some Notes on Recent American Fiction," *Encounter*, Vol. XXI, No. 5, November 1963, p. 29.
53. *Ibid.*, p. 28.
54. "The Sealed Treasure," p. 9.
55. *Ibid.*
56. Saul Bellow, "Arias," *The Noble Savage*, IV (Chicago, 1960), p. 5.
57. Saul Bellow, "Bunuel's Unsparing Vision," *Horizon*, V (November, 1962), p. 112.
58. "The Thinking Man's Wasteland," p. 20.
59. "A Conversation with Saul Bellow," p. 11.
60. Saul Bellow, "Culture Now : Some Animadversions, Some Laughs," *Modern Occasions*, Vol. I, No. 2, Winter 1971, p. 170.
61. *Ibid.*, p. 177.
62. *Ibid.*
63. *Ibid*, p. 178.

CHAPTER 2
FICTIONAL METHOD

1. "Culture Now," p. 178.
2. "Writers and Morals," p. 13.
3. *Ibid.*
4. *Ibid.*, p. 14.
5. *Ibid.*, p. 15.
6. Norman Mailer, "The White Negro," *Advertisements for Myself* (London, 1968), p. 286.
7. *Ibid.*
8. Sylvia Plath, *The Bell Jar* (London, 1971).
9. *Ibid.*, p. 88.
10. *Ibid.*, p. 123.
11. *Ibid.*, p. 130.
12. *Ibid.*, p. 128.
13. *Ibid.*, p. 129.
14. Saul Bellow, "The Art of Going it Alone," *Horizon*, 5 (September, 1962), p. 110.
15. Quoted from a Profile of Bellow in *Saturday Review*, September 19, 1964, p. 38.
16. Saul Bellow, *Mosby's Memoirs* (New York, 1969), p. 162.
17. *Ibid.*, p. 156.
18. "Two Faces for a Hostile World," rev. of Jean Dutourd's *Five A.M.*, pp. 4-5.
19. The term "prosocial" is used by Elizabeth Z. Johnson while drawing a distinction between contrasocial and prosocial aggression. See, E. Johnson, "Attitudes of children toward authority as projected in their doll play at two age levels," Unpublished doctoral dissertation, Harvard University, 1951.
20. Lauren G. Wispe, "Positive Forms of Social Behaviour : An Overview," *The Journal of Social Issues*, Vol. 28, No. 3, 1972, p. 1.
21. *Ibid.*, p. 7.
22. O.E. Sperling "A Psychoanalytic Study of Social-mindedness," *The Psychoanalytic Quarterly*, 1955, 24, p. 257.
23. Langdon Gilkey, *Time*, April 8, 1966, p. 52.
24. Nathan A. Scott, Jr., "Criticism and the Religious Horizon," mimeographed paper, p. 24-25.
25. Martin Buber, *Eclipse of God* (New York, 1952), p. 11.
26. Gerhard Ebeling, *The Nature of Faith*, trans. Ronald Gregor Smith (Philadelphia, 1961), pp. 159-160.
27. Maxwell Geismar, "Saul Bellow : Novelist of the Intellectuals," *Saul Bellow and the Critics*, ed. Irving Malin (London, 1967), p. 17.
28. George Woodcock, "Ignazio Silone," *Focus Two*, ed. B. Rajan and Andrew Pearse (London, 1946), p. 40.
29. Maxwell Geismar, "The Great *Herzog* Schande," *The Minority of One*, VI (December 1946), p. 30.

NOTES

30. Nathan A. Scott, Jr., "Bellow's Vision of the 'Axial Lines," *Three American Moralists : Mailer, Bellow, Trilling* (Notre Dame, 1973) p. 105.
31. *Ibid.*, p. 146.
32. T.S. Eliot, "The Perfect Critic," *The Sacred Wood* (London, 1964), pp. 2-7.
33. Nicolas Berdyaev, *Dostoievsky*, trans. Donald Attwater (New York, 1934).
34. Will Durant, *The Life of Greece*, Vol. II of *The Story of Civilization* (New York, 1966), p. 368.
35. Max F. Schulz, *Radical Sophistication: Studies in Contemporary Jewish-American Novelists* (Athens, Ohio, 1969), p. 110.
36. Ingmar Bergman, "Introduction," *Four Screenplays of Ingmar Bergman*, trans. Lars Malmstrom and David Kusher (New York, 1966), p. xxi.
37. Saul Bellow, "Literature," *The Great Ideas Today* (New York, 1963), pp. 171-173.
38. *Ibid.*
39. *Ibid.*
40. Saul Bellow ed., *Great Jewish Short Stories* (New York, 1966), p. 12.
41. *Ibid.*

CHAPTER 3

THE VICTIMS

1. Henri F. Ellenberger, "A Clinical Introduction to Psychiatric Phenomenology and Existential Analysis," *Existence*, ed. Rollo May, Ernest Angel, Henri F. Ellenberger (New York, 1958), p. 100.
2. Saul Bellow, "Two Morning Monologues," *Partisan Review*, Vol. VIII, No. 3, May-June 1941, pp. 230-231.
3. *Ibtd.*, p. 234-235.
4. *Ibid.*, p. 234.

DANGLING MAN

1. "Saul Bellow : An Interview," p. 62.
2. Frank Kermode, *Continuities* (London, 1968), pp. 223-224.
3. Edmund Wilson, *The New Yorker*, 20 (April 1, 1944), p. 78.
4. Time, 43 (May 8, 1944), p. 104.
5. "Saul Bellow : An Interview," p. 56.
6. *Ibid.*, p. 55.
7. Robert Gorham Davis, "The American Individualist Tradition : Bellow and Styron," *The Creative Present*, ed. Nona Balakian and Charles Simmons (New York, 1963), p. 116.
8. See, for example, Maxwell Geismar, "Saul Bellow : Novelist of the Intellectuals," p. 11.
9. Chester E. Eisinger, *Fiction of the Forties* (Chicago, 1963), p. 345.

10. Reuben Frank, "Saul Bellow : The Evolution of a Contemporary Novelist," *Western Review*, 18 (Winter, 1954), p. 103.
11. "Distractions of a Fiction Writer," p. 30.
12. Fyodor Dostoevsky, *Notes from Underground, Poor People, The Friend of the Family*, trans. Constance Garnett (New York, 1965).
13. David D. Galloway, *The Absurd Hero in American Fiction: Updike, Styron, Bellow, Salinger*, (Austin, 1966), p. 84.
14. Albert Camus, *The Stranger*, trans. Stuart Gilbert (New York, 1946).
15. *The Absurd Hero in American Fiction*, p. 84.
16. Erich Fromm, *Escape from Freedom* (New York, 1965), pp. 284.
17. *Ibid.*, pp. 161-162.
18. Jean Paul Sartre, *Nausea*, trans. Robert Baldick (Harmondsworth, 1966). For Bellow's reaction to *Nausea* see *To Jerusalem and Back* (Harmondsworth, 1977), p .119.
19. *Ibid.*, pp. 211-212.
20. *Ibid.*, pp. 223.

SEIZE THE DAY

1. Daniel Weiss, "Caliban on Prospero : A Psychoanalytic Study on the Novel *Seize the Day*, by Saul Bellow," *Saul Bellow and the Critics*, ed. Irving Malin, pp. 114-141.
2. *Saul Bellow : In Defense of Man*, pp. 69-74.
3. "Caliban on Prospero," p. 121.
4. *Ibid.*, p. 120.
5. *Saul Bellow : In Defense of Man*, p. 70.
6. "The Writer as Moralist," p. 62.
7. *Ibid.*
8. "Caliban on Prospero," p. 136.
9. *Saul Bellow : In Defense of Man*, p. 74.
10. "Caliban on Prospero," p. 136.
11. *Saul Bellow : In Defense of Man*, p. 106.

CHAPTER 4

THE ADVENTURERS
THE ADVENTURES OF AUGIE MARCH

1. Bruce Cook, "Saul Bellow : A Mood of Protest," *Perspective*, XII (February 1963), pp. 49-50.
2. Harvey Breit, "Talk with Saul Bellow," *New York Times Book Review*, LXIII (September 20, 1953,) p. 20.
3. Robert Alter, *Rogue's Progress* (Cambridge, Mass., 1964), p. 124.
4. "Saul Bellow: A Mood of Protest," p. 50.
5. Robert Penn Warren, *New Republic*, CXXIX (November 2, 1953), pp. 22-23.

6. Thomas Mann, *The Magic Mountain*, trans. H.T. Lowe-Porter (Harmondsworth, 1976).
7. Saul Bellow, "Trip to Galena," *Partisan Review*, XVII (November, 1950), pp. 779-94.
8. *Ibid.*, p. 789.
9. Saul Bellow, "How I wrote Augie March's Story," *New York Times Book Review*, LIX (January 31, 1954), p. 3.
10. "Saul Bellow : A Mood of Protest," p. 49.
11. *Ibid.*
12. Nina Steers, "Successor to Faulkner ?" *Show*, IV (September, 1964), p. 38.
13. Leslie Fiedler, "Saul Bellow," *Prairie Schooner*, XXXI (Summer, 1957), p. 109.
14. Richard Chase, "The Adventures of Saul Bellow : Progress of a Novelist," *Commentary*, XXVII (April 1956), p. 327.

CHAPTER 5
THE SURVIVORS

1. Bernard Malamud, *The Fixer* (Harmondsworth, 1967).
2. Alexander Solzhenitsyn, *One Day in the Life of Ivan Denisovich*, trans. Max Hayward and Ronald Hingley (New York, 1970).
3. Terence Des Pres, "The Survivor : On the Ethics of Survival in Extremity," *Encounter*, Vol. XXXVII, No. 3, September 1971, p. 7.
4. *Ibid.*, pp. 10-11.
5. *Ibid.*, p. 7.
6. *Ibid.*, p 6.
7. For a detailed account of the parallels between the circumstances of Schwartz's life and the plot of *Humboldt's Gift*, see James Atlas, *Delmore Schwartz : The Life of an American Poet* (New York, 1977). Also see, Louis Simpson, "Ghost of Delmore Schwartz," *New York Times Magazine*, December 7, 1975, pp. 38-56.

HERZOG

1. Northrop Frye, *Anatomy of Criticism* (New York, 1969), p. 309.
2. *Ibid.*, p. 311.
3. *Ibid.*, p. 309.
4. The relevant reference to Kierkegaard occurs in *Mr. Sammler's Planet*, pp. 62.
5. "Saul Bellow : An Interview," p. 69.
6. *Ibid.*, pp. 69-70.
7. John W. Aldridge, "The Complacency of Herzog," *Saul Bellow and the Critics*, ed. Irving Malin, p. 208.
8. *Ibid.*, pp. 208-209.
9. Earl Rovit, "Bellow in Occupancy," *Ibid.*, p. 179.

10. Heinrich Boll, *The Clown*, trans. Leila Vennewitz (London, 1963).
11. *Ibid.*, p. 110.
12. *Ibid.*, p. 21.
13. Peter M. Axthelm, *The Modern Confessional Novel* (New Haven, 1967), p. 6.

MR. SAMMLER'S PLANET

1. Irving Howe, *New Republic*, 151 (September 19, 1964), pp. 21-26.
2. "A Conversation with Saul Bellow," p. 8.
3. Keith Opdahl, *Commonweal*, February 13, 1970, p. 537.
4. "A Conversation with Saul Bellow," p. 8.
5. W.B. Yeats, *Selected Poems* (London, 1962), p. 104.
6. "In Search of Order," rev. of *Mr. Sammler's Planet*, *The Times Literary Supplement*, July 9, 1970, pp. 749-750.
7. Benjamin DeMott, "Saul Bellow and the Dogmas of Possibility," *Saturday Review*, February 7, 1970, pp. 25-28, 37.
8. Anatole Broyard, "Mr. Sammler's Planet," *New York Times Book Review*, February 1, 1970, p. 40.
9. Edward Grossman, "The Bitterness of Saul Bellow," *Midstream*, August-September 1970, pp. 3-15.
10. *Commonweal*, February 13, 1970, p. 537.
11. *Saul Bellow : In Defense of Man*, pp. 254-260.
12. "A Conversation with Saul Bellow," p. 9.
13. *Ibid.*, p. 9.
14. *Ibid.*, p. 9.
15. Paul Tillich, *The Courage to Be* (New Haven, 1968), pp. 171-178.
16. *Ibid.*, p. 172.
17. *Ibid.*
18. *Ibid.*, p. 173.
19. "Saul Bellow : An Interview," p. 64.
20. "A Conversation with Saul Bellow," p. 11.
21. "Saul Bellow : An Interview," pp. 65-66.
22. Quoted in "A Conversation with Saul Bellow," p. 11.

CONCLUSION

TOWARD A MYSTIQUE OF SAUL BELLOW

1. *Sincerity and Authenticity*, p. 167.
2. *Ibid*, p. 168.
3. *Ibid.*, p. 169.
4. *Ibid.*, p. 171.
5. *Ibid.*
6. "The Nobel Lecture," p. 321.
7. "The Gonzaga Manuscripts," *Mosby's Memoirs*, pp. 109-137.
8. Eric Hoffer, *The True Believer* (New York, 1951).
9. "Saul Bellow : An Interview," p. 72.
10. *Ibid.*, p. 73.

Select Bibliography

Abbreviations used:
- NYTBR   for New York Times Book Review
- NYHTBR for New York Herald Tribune Book Review
- SRL   for Saturday Review of Literature
- TLS   for Times Literary Supplement

This is a short bibliography restricted mainly to items used in this study. For a detailed listing of works by and on Saul Bellow a reference may be made to Marianne Nault, *Saul Bellow: His Works and His Critics: An Annotated International Bibliography* (New York, 1971), p. 191.

LONGER WORKS

Dangling Man. New York: Vanguard, 1944.
The Victim. New York: Vanguard, 1947.
The Adventures of Augie March. New York: Viking Press, 1953.
Seize the Day. New York: Viking Press, 1956.
Henderson the Rain King. New York: Viking Press, 1959.
Herzog. New York: Viking Press, 1964.
The Last Analysis (play). New York: Viking Press, 1965.
Mosby's Memoirs and Other Stories. New York: Viking Press, 1968.
Mr. Sammler's Planet. New York: Viking Press, 1970.
Humboldt's Gift. New York: Viking Press, 1975.
To Jerusalem and Back. Harmondsworth: Penguin Books, 1977.

SHORT FICTION

1941 "Two Morning Monologues," *Partisan Review*, 8 (May-

June, 1941), 230-36.

1942 "The Mexican General," *Partisan Review*, 9 (May-June, 1942), 178-94.

1949 "Sermon by Doctor Pep," *Partisan Review*, 16 (May 1949), 455-62.

"Dora," Harper's Bazaar, 83 (November 1949), 118, 188-90, 198-99.

1950 "Trip to Galena," *Partisan Review*, 17 (November-December 1950), 779-94.

1951 "Looking for Mr. Green," *Commentary*, 17 (March 1951), 251-61.

"By the Rock Wall," *Harper's Bazaar*, 85 (April 1951), 135, 205, 207-8, 214-16.

"Address by Gooley MacDowell to the Hasbeens Club of Chicago," *Hudson Review*, 4 (Summer 1951), 222-27.

"The Coblins," *Sewanee Review*, 59 (Autumn 1951), 635-53.

1954 "The Wrecker" (play), *New World Writing*, 6 (1954), 261-87.

1955 "A Father-to-Be," *The New Yorker*, 30 (Febuary 5, 1955), 26-30.

1956 "The Gonzaga Manuscripts," *Discovery No 4*, ed. Vance Bourjaily (New York, 1956).

1958 "Leaving the Yellow House," *Esquire*, 49 (January 1958), 112-26.

1965 "A Wen" (play), *Esquire*, 63 (January 1965), 72-74, 111.

REVIEWS

"Beatrice Webb's America", *Nation*, 197 (September 7, 1963), 116.

"Dreiser and the Triumph of Art," *Commentary*, 11 (May 1951), 502-3.

"Gide as Autobiographer," *New Leader*, June 4, 1951, p. 24.

"Hemingway and the Image of Man," *Partisan Review*, 20 (May-June 1953), 338-42.

"Italian Fiction: Without Hope," *New Leader*, December 11, 1950, 21-22.

"Laughter in the Ghetto," *SRL*, 36 (May 30, 1953), 15.

"Movies," *Horizon*, 5 (September 1962), 108-10.

"Movies," *Horizon*, 5 (November 1962), 110-12.
"Movies," *Horizon*, 5 (January 1963), 111-13.
"Movies," *Horizon*, 5 (March 1963), 109-11.
"A Personal Record," *New Republic*, 130 (February 22, 1954), 20.
"Pleasure and Pains of Playgoing," *Partisan Review*, 21 (May-June 1954), 312-17.
"Rabbi's Boy in Edinburgh," *SRL*, 39 (March 24, 1956), 19.
"The Riddle of Shakespeare's Sonnets," *The Griffin*, 11 (June 1962), 4-8.
"The Swamp of Prosperity," *Commentary*, 38 (July 1959), 77-79.
"Two Faces of a Hostile World," *NYTBR*, 61 (August 26, 1956), 4-5.
"The Uses of Adversity," *The Reporter*, 21 (October 1, 1959), 42-44.

ARTICLES

"Culture Now: Some Animadversions, Some Laughs," *Modern Occasions*, 1, No. 2 (Winter 1971), 162-178.
"Deep Readers of the World, Beware!" *NYTBR*, 64 (February 15, 1959), 1, 34.
"Distractions of a Fiction Writer," *The Living Novel*, ed. Granville Hicks (New York, 1957), 1-20.
"Foreword," John Berryman, *Recovery*, (New York, 1973).
"Foreword," Isaac Rosenfeld, *An Age of Enormity*, ed. Theodore Solotaroff (Cleveland, Ohio, 1962).
"The French as Dostoevsky Saw Them," *New Republic*, 132 (May 23, 1955), 17-20.
"How I Wrote Augie March's Story," *NYTBR*, 59 (January 31, 1954), 3, 17.
"Illinois Journey," *Holiday*, 22 (September 1959), 62, 102-7.
"Introduction," *Great Jewish Short Stories*, ed. Saul Bellow (New York: Dell, 1963), 9-16.
"Isaac Rosenfeld," *Partisan Review*, 23 (Fall 1956), 565-67.
"The Jewish Writer and the English Literary Tradition," *Commentary*, 8 (October 1949), 366-67.
"Literary Notes on Khruschev," *Esquire*, 55 (March 1961), 106-7.
"Literature," *The Great Ideas Today* (New York: Encyclopaedia Britannica Inc., 1963), 135-79.

"Machines and Story Books: Literature in the Age of Technology," *Harper's*, 249, No. 1491 (August 1974), 48-59.

"My Man Bummidge," *New York Times*, September 27, 1964, Section 2, 1.

"The Noble Lecture," *The American Scholar*, 46, No. 3 (Summer 1977), 316-325.

"Recent American Fiction," Lecture delivered under the auspices of the Gertrude Clarke Whittal Poetry and Literature Fund (Washington: Library of Congress, 1963), *Encounter*, 21 (November 1963), 22-29.

"The Sealed Treasure," *The Open Form*, ed. Alfred Kazin (New York, 1961), 3-9.

"Spanish Letter," *Partisan Review*, 15 (February 1948), 217-30.

"A Talk with the Yellow Kid," *The Reporter*, 15 (September 6, 1956), 41-44.

"Thinking Man's Wasteland" (Excerpt from address), *Saturday Review*, 48 (April 3, 1965), 20.

Translation of I.B. Singer's "Gimpel the Fool," *Partisan Review*, 20 (May-June, 1953), 300-13.

"The University as Villain," *Nation*, 185 (November 16, 1957), 361-63.

"A World Too Much With Us," *Critical Inquiry*, 2. No. 1 (Autumn 1975), 1-9.

"Where Do We Go from Here: The Future of Fiction," *Michigan Quarterly Review*, 1 (Winter 1962), 27-33.

"A Word from Writer Directly to Reader," *Fiction of the Fifties*, ed. Herbert Gold (New York 1959), 19.

"The Writer and the Audience," *Perspectives USA*, 9 (Autumn 1954), 99-102.

"The Writer as Moralist," *Atlantic*, 211 (March 1963), 58-62.

"Writers and Morals," Unpublished article in Saul Bellow papers at the Joseph Regenstein Library, University of Chicago, Chicago.

THE NOBLE SAVAGE

Edited by Saul Bellow, this periodical contains unsigned articles by him.

"Number One," eds. Saul Bellow, Keith Botsford, and Jack Ludwig (New York, 1960).

"Number Two," eds. Saul Bellow, Keith Botsford, and Jack Ludwig (New York, 1960).
"Number Three," eds. Saul Bellow and Keith Botsford (New York, 1961).
"Number Four," eds. Saul Bellow and Keith Botsford (New York, 1961).
"Number Five," eds. Saul Bellow, Keith Botsford, and Aaron Asher (New York, 1962).

BIOGRAPHICAL MATERIAL AND INTERVIEWS

Bellow on Himself and America," *Jerusalem Post*, No. 507, July 13, 1970.
Breit, Harvey, "Saul Bellow," *The Writer Observed* (New York, 1961), 176-78.
Harper, G.L., "Saul Bellow: An Interview," *Paris Review*, 36 (Winter 1966), 49-73.
Henry, Jim Douglas, "Mystic Trade," *The Listener*, May 22, 1969.
Howard, Jane, "Saul Bellow Considers this Planet," *Life*, 68, No. 12 (April 3, 1970), 57-60.
Kazin, Alfred, "My Friend Saul Bellow," *The Atlantic*, 215 (January 1965), 51-54.
Kulshrestha, Chirantan, *The Saul Bellow Estate* (Calcutta, 1976).
——, "An Indian Writer Remembers Saul Bellow," *Span*, Vol. XIX, No.2, February 1977, 31-33.
——, "Meeting Saul Bellow," *The American Review*, 16, No. 3 (April 1972), 77-84.
——, "A Conversation with Saul Bellow," *Chicago Review*, 23, No. 4 and 24, No. 1, 7-15.
Kunitz, Stanley, J., ed. *Twentieth Century Authors*, First Supplement (New York, 1955), 72-73.
"Saul Bellow: An Interview," *Wisconsin Studies in Contemporary Literature*, 6 (Summer 1965), 156-60.
Steers, Nina A., "Successor to Faulkner ?" *Show*, 4 (September 1964), 36-38.

GENERAL CRITICISM

Aldridge, John W., "The Society of Three Novels," *In Search*

of Heresy (New York, 1956).
Alter, Robert, *Rouge's Progress: Studies in the Picaresque Novel* (Cambridge, Mass., 1964).
——, "The Stature of Saul Bellow," *Midstream*, 10 (December 1964), 3-15.
Atlas, James, *Delmore Schwartz: The Life of an American Poet* (New York, 1977).
Auerbach, Erich, *Mimesis* (New York, 1957).
Axthelm, Peter M., *The Modern Confessional Novel* (New Haven, 1967).
Baumbach, Jonathan, *The Landscape of Nightmare* (New York, 1965), 35-54.
Berdyaev, Nicolas, *Dostoievsky*, trans., Donald Attwater (New York, 1934).
Bergler, Edmund, "Writers of Half-Talent," *American Imago*, 14 (Summer 1957), 155-64.
Bergman, Ingmar, *Four Screenplays of Ingmar Bergman*, trans. Lars Malmstrom and David Kusher (New York, 1966).
Boyers, Robert, "Nature and Social Reality in Bellow's Sammler," *The Critical Quarterly*, 15, No. 3 (Autumn 1973), 251-271.
Bradbury, Malcolm, "Saul Bellow's *The Victim*," *The Critical Quarterly*, 5 (Summer 1963), 119-27.
——, "Saul Bellow and the Naturalist Tradition," *Review of English Literature*, 4 (October 1963), 80-92.
Buber, Martin, *Eclipse of God* (New York 1952).
Chase, Richard, "The Adventures of Saul Bellow: Progress of a Novelist," *Commentary*, 27 (April 1959), 323-30.
Clayton, John J., *Saul Bellow: In Defense of Man* (Bloomington, 1971).
Cohen, Sarah Blacher, *Saul Bellow's Enigmatic Laughter* (Urbana, 1974).
Cook, Bruce, "Saul Bellow : A Mood of Protest," *Perspective*, 12 (February 1963), 47-50.
Crozier, R.D., "Theme in *Augie March*," *Critique*, 7 (Spring 1965), 18-32.
Davis, Robert G., "The American Individualist Tradition : Bellow and Styron," *The Creative Present*, ed. N. Balakian and C. Simmons (Garden City, N (Y.), 1963), 111-41.
Des Pres, Terence, "The Survivor: On the Ethics of Survival in

SELECT BIBLIOGRAPHY

Extremity," *Encounter*, 37, No. 3 (September 1971), 3-19.

Donoghue, Denis, "Commitment and the Dangling Man," *Studies*, 53 (Summer 1964), 174-87.

Durant, Will, *The Life of Greece*, Vol. II of *The Story of Civilization* (New York, 1967).

Dutton, Robert E., *Saul Bellow* (New York, 1971).

Ebeling, Gerhard, *The Nature of Faith*, trans. Ronald Gregor Smith (Philadelphia, 1961).

Eisinger, Chester E., *Fiction of the Forties* (Chicago, 1963), 341-62.

Eliot, T.S., *The Sacred Wood* (London, 1964).

——, *The Use of Poetry and the Use of Criticism* (London, 1930).

Fiedler, Leslie A., "The Breakthrough: The American Jewish Novelist and the Fictional Image of the Jew," *Midstream*, 4 (Winter 1958), 15-35. Also in *Recent American Fiction: Some Critical Views*, ed. Joseph J. Waldmeir (Boston, 1963), 84-109.

——, *Love and Death in the American Novel* (New York, 1960), 360.

——, "Saul Bellow," *Prairie Schooner*, 3 (Summer 1957), 103-10. Also in *The Modern Critical Spectrum*, ed. Gerald J. Goldberg and Nancy M. Goldberg (Englewood Cliffs, N.J.: 1962), 155-61.

Fisch, Harold, "The Hero as Jew: Reflection on *Herzog*," *Judaism*, 17, No. 1 (Winter 1968), 42-54.

Flaubert, Gustave, *Letters*, ed. Richard Rumbold (London, 1950).

Frank, Reuben, "Saul Bellow: The Evolution of a Contemporary Novelist." *Western Review*, 18 (Winter 1954), 101-12.

Freedman, Ralph, "Saul Bellow: The Illusion of Environment," *Wisconsin Studies in Contemporary Literature*, 1 (Winter 1954), 50-65.

Frye, Northrop, *Anatomy of Criticism* (New York, 1969).

Galloway, David D., *The Absurd Hero in American Fiction* (Austin, 1966).

Geismar, Maxwell, "Saul Bellow: Novelist of the Intellectuals," *American Moderns: From Rebellion to Conformity* (New Yark, 1958), 210-24.

Gold, Herbert, "Introduction," *Fiction of the Fifties*, ed. Herbert Gold (New York, 1959), 7-17. Reprinted in "Fiction of the Fifties," *Hudson Review*, 12 (Summer 1959), 192-201; in *Recent American Fiction*, ed. Joseph J. Waldmeir (Boston, 1963), 36-44.

Goldberg, Gerald J., "Life's Customer, Augie March," *Critique*, 3 (Summer 1960), 15-27.

Grossman, Edward, "The Bitterness of Saul Bellow," *Midstream*, August-September 1970, 3-15.

Guttmann, Allen, *The Jewish Writer in America* (New York, 1971).

Handy, William J., "Saul Bellow and the Naturalistic Hero," *Texas Studies in Literature and Language*, 5 (Winter 1964), 538-45.

Hassan, Ihab H., *Radical Innocence : Studies in the Contemporary American Novel* (New York, 1966), 290-324.

Hoffman, Frederick J., "The Fool of Experience," *Contemporary American Novelists*, ed. Harry T. Moore (Carbondale, 256, 1964), 80-94.

———, *The Modern Novel in America : 1900-1950*. (Chicago, 1951), 188-89.

Hoffer, Eric, *The True Believer* (New York, 1951).

Howe, Irving, "Mass Society and Post-Modern Fiction," *Partisan Review*, 26 (Summer 1959), 420-36. Reprinted in *A World More Attractive* (New York, 1963), 77-97, in *Recent American Fiction*, ed. Joseph J. Waldmeir (Boston, 1963), 3-17.

Hughes, Daniel, "Reality and the Hero : Lolita and Henderson the Rain King," *Modern Fiction Studies*, 6 (Winter 1960-61), 345-64.

Josipovici, Gabriel, *The World and the Book* (Stanford, 1971).

Kazin, Alfred, " The World of Saul Bellow," *The Griffin*, June, 1959, pp. 4-9. Also in *Contemporaries* (Boston, 1962), 217-23.

———, "Bright Book of Life : American Novelists and Storytellers from Hemingway to Mailer* (Bombay, 1973).

Kermode, Frank, *Continuities* (London 1968).

Klein, Marcus, "A Discipline of Nobility: Saul Bellow's Fiction," *After Alienation* (New York, 1962), 33-70.

Lehan, Richard, "Existentialism in Recent American Fiction : The Demonic Quest," *Taxas Studies in Literature and Language*, 1 (Spring 1959), 181-202.

Levenson, J.C., "Bellow's Dangling Men," *Critique*, 3 (Summer 1960), 3-14.

Levine, Paul, "Saul Bellow : The Affirmation of the Philosophical Fool," *Perspective*, 19 (Winter 1959), 163-76.
Lewis, R.W.B., *The American Adam* (Chicago, 1955), 199-200.
——, *The Picaresque Saint* (Philadelphia, 1958).
Ludwig, Jack, *Recent American Novelists* (Minneapolis, Minn., 1962).
Mailer, Norman, *Advertisements for Myself* (New York, 1966), 426-36.
——, "Modes and Mutations : Quick Comments on the Modern American Novel," *Commentary*, 41 (March 1966), 37-40.
Malin, Irving, ed. *Saul Bellow and the Critics* (New York, 1967).
——, *Saul Bellow's Fiction* (Carbondale,1969).
May, Rollo, etc. ed. *Existence* (New York, 1958).
Opdahl, Keith Michael, *The Novels of Saul Bellow : An Introduction* (University Park, Pennsylvania, 1967).
Podhoretz, Norman, *Doings and Undoings* (New York, 1964), 205-27.
Porter, Gilbert, *Whence The Power ? The Artistry and Humanity of Saul Bellow* (Columbia, 1974).
Quinton, Anthony, "The Adventures of Saul Bellow," *London Magazine*, 6 (December 1959), 55-59.
Rajan, B., etc., ed. *Focus Two* (London, 1946).
Rans, Geoffrey, "The Novels of Saul Bellow," *Review of English Literature*, 3 (October 1963), 18-30.
Rosenberg, Harold, *The Anxious Object* (New York, 1969).
——, *Discovering the Present* (Chicago, 1973).
Ross, Theodore J., "Notes on Saul Bellow," *Chicago Jewish Forum*, 18 (Fall 1959), 21-27.
Rovit, Earl, *Saul Bellow* (Minneapolis, 1967).
——, *Saul Bellow : A Collection of Critical Essays* (Englewood Cliffs, N.J., 1975).
Salmagundi, No. 30, Summer 1975 (Special Number on "Saul Bellow : Literature and Culture").
Salter, D.P.M., "Optimism and Reaction in Saul Bellow's Recent Work," *The Critical Quarterly*, 14, No. 1 (Spring 1972), 57-66.
Samuel, Maurice, "My Friend, the Late Moses Herzog," *Midstream*, 12 (April 1966), 3-25.
Scheer-Schazler, Brigitte; *Saul Bellow* (New York, 1972).

Schulz, Max F., *Radical Sophistication* (Athens, 1969).
Scott, Jr., Nathan A., *Three American Moralists : Mailer, Bellow, Trilling* (Notre Dame, 1973).
Simpson, Louis, "Ghost of Delmore Schwartz," *New York Times Magazine*, December 7, 1975, pp. 38-56.
Tanner, Tony, *Saul Bellow* (Edinburgh, 1965).
——, *City of Words : American Fiction* (1950-70), (New York, 1971).
Tillich, Paul, *The Courage to Be* (New Haven, 1968).
Trilling, Lionel, *Beyond Culture* (New York, 1965).
——, *Sincerity and Authenticity* (Cambridge, Mass., 1973).
Weinberg, Helen, *The New Novel in America : The Kafkan Mode in Contemporary Fiction* (Ithaca, 1970).
Young, J.D., "Bellow's View of the Heart," *Critique*, 7 (Spring 1965), 5-17.

Index

Adorno, Theodor, 140
Aldridge, John W., 127
Algern, Nelson, 54
Alter, Robert, 24, 98
Auerbach Erich, 27
Axthelm, Peter M., 131

Baldwin, James, 15, 36
Bellow, Saul,
   On the nature and function of art, 26-39
   Fictional Method, 40-60
   Private Papers, 13-14
   Seize the Day and the Bellow Chronology, 19-23
   Individual Novels, 61-149
   Jewishness, 11-13, 23-25
   Mystique, 150-154
Berdyaev, Nicolas, 56
Bergman, Ingmar, 58
Berkowitz, L., 50
Bhave, Vinoba, 10
Boll, Heinrich, 130-132
Brown, Norman O., 38, 140, 150, 153
Buber, Martin, 53, 120
Burroughs, William, 15

Campbell, D.T., 50
Camus, Albert 27, 75
Capote, Truman, 15
Chase, Richard, 107
Clayton, John J., 85-87, 91-93, 137
Collingwood, R.G., 38

Darley, J., 50
Davis, Robert Gorham, 65-66
De Quincey, 22
Des Pres, Terence, 109
Donleavy, J.P., 36
Dostoevski, F., 13, 56, 70-71, 77
Dreiser, Theodore, 13, 54
Durant, Will, 56
Dutourd, Jean, 34

Ebeling, Gerhard, 53
Eckhardt, Meister, 140, 148
Eisinger, Chester, 67
Eliot, T.S., 26, 56
Ellenberger, Henri F., 61
Emerson, Ralph Waldo, 38
Engel, Morris, 47

Farrell, James T., 54
Faulkner, William, 27
Fiedler, Leslie A., 19, 29, 107
Flaubert, Gustave, 26, 29
Foucault, M, 150, 153
Frank, Reuben, 68
Fromm, Erich, 75, 77
Frye, Northrop, 114

Galloway, David D., 75
Gebsattel, Von, 61
Geismar, Maxwell, 54, 55
Gide, Andre, 26
Gilkey, Langdon, 53
Gouldner, A, 50

Grossman, Edward, 137
Guttmann, Allen, 24

Hegel, Georg Wilhelm Friedrich, 123
Heidegger, Martin, 118, 122, 123
Hobbes, Thomas, 70
Hoffer, Eric, 153
Howe, Irving, 132

Jones, James, 36
Joyce, James, 26, 27

Kermode, Frank, 64
Kierkegaard, Soren, 46, 121, 142

Laing, R.D., 150, 153
Latane, B., 50
Lewis, R.W.B., 27

Mailer, Norman, 15, 43, 153
Malamud, Bernard, 15, 24
Malin, Irving, 24
Malraux, Andre, 27
Mann, Thomas, 13, 27, 101
Marcuse, Herbert, 140
Marx, Karl, 123, 140
Montaigne, M.E., 119
Moravia, Alberto, 27

O'Hara, John, 36
Opdahl, Keith M., 133, 137
Oppenheimer, Franz, 140
Ortega y Gasset, Jose, 140

Pascal, Blaise, 119
Plath, Sylvia, 44-45, 46, 153
Proudhon, Pierre Joseph, 123
Proust, Marcel, 27

Rosenberg, Harold, 24, 25, 31, 32
Roth, Philip, 15, 36

Rovit, Earl, 129

Salinger, J.D., 15
Sartre, Jean-Paul, 76-77
Scheler, Max, 140
Schulz, Max F., 58
Scott, Jr., Nathan A., 53, 55-56
Shakespeare, William, 10
Shils, Edward, 14
Shilone, Ignazio, 27, 54
Slate, Hymen, 56
Socrates, 56
Spengler, Oswald, 123
Sperling, O E., 123
Stuart-Forbes, 9-10
Symons, Arthur, 56

Tanner, Tony, 16
Tillich, Paul, 147-148
Tolstoy, Leo, 41
Trilling, Lionel, 32-33, 150-151

Updike, John, 36

Valery, Paul, 140

Warren, Robert Penn, 101
Weber, Max 140
Weinberg, Helen, 19, 20
Weiss, Daniel, 85-87, 91-93
Wells, H.G., 133, 135, 139, 145
West, Ray B., 19
Wilson, Edmund, 64
Wispe, Lauren G., 50-51
Wolfert, Ira, 54
Woodcock, George, 54
Woolf, Virginia, 27

Yeats, W.B., 133